www.thebigbookofcareersdoodles.com

Testimonials

"This book is a breath of fresh air in a world of information overload. It takes complex career management concepts and turns them into actionable insights anyone can apply. It will be within easy reach in my resource library for years to come."

Gillian Kelly. LinkedIn Top Voice. Director, Outplacement Australia

"As a global career development professional, I practice and advocate that career development is a civic right for people around the globe. I am happy to share testimonial and recommendation for 'The Big Book of Career Doodles'. Heartiest Congratulations to Naishadh Gadani for initiating a creative and fun book which is needed in current times. The drawings and visual analogies have thoughtfully been chosen and the narrative with each image by notable career development experts from around the globe further endorses the credibility of the book and its reach to an inclusive global audience. The book covers very important topics in our career development sector such as Job Search, Career Development/ Transition, Social Media/Personal Branding, and Self-Development. The content of the book also promotes inclusive learners that have a visual and kinesthetic style of learning. I highly recommend this book to university students, career development centers, and society at large. Let's continue to collectively advocate that 'career development is the change we wish to see in the world."

Raza Abbas - Global Multi Awards Cross-Cultural Career Specialist.

"This comprehensive, jam-packed, visually stunning book contains everything you need to get your career on the move! It's wonderfully illustrated with expert advice from career professionals. I have enjoyed Naishadh's regular doodles on LinkedIn for some time. This brings together a superb collection of career wisdom in enjoyable sketches that gets to the heart of motivating you to look at something differently and take a new step forward. These entertaining doodles with concise advice have everything you need to both look at a situation with new eyes and be amused at the same time. It nicely captures career development from the head and the heart. Congratulations Naishadh on creating a truly creative masterpiece that will resonate with people around the world who want to shine at being the best at what they do."

Warren Frehse, Career Growth and Transition Coach, Author.

The Big Book of Career Doodles

87 visual ideas to inspire a great career!

Publishing Information

Cover design by Brijmohan Chourasiya
Printed and bound in Australia by

ISBN: 978-0-6455685-0-9

ISBN 978-0-6455685-0-9

9 780645 568509 >

www.thebigbookofcareerdoodles.com

This book was written on the lands of the Wurundjeri people of the Kulin nation, who I would like to acknowledge as the Traditional Custodians of their country. I pay my respects to the Elders past and present, and celebrate their histories, tradition, and living cultures of Aboriginal and Torres Strait Islander people on the land.

Dedicated to:

My family, consisting of Nildhara, Kshitij (Krish), and Shivam, have been my unwavering support system throughout this journey. But let's not forget the real MVP - our furry friend Buddy. Walking him not only kept us active but also sparked countless doodle ideas in my head.

And to my Mom and Dad, thank you for letting me pursue my interests, even if it's still a bit of a mystery to you. Rest assured, my work is making a positive impact on the community.

An Open Letter to People Who Care About Their Careers.

Have you ever thought that you could "think" your way out of a sticky job situation?

Or you needed to "think" harder to solve a career decision?

Tough, isn't it?

The problem with words is that they force us into thinking in a linear way – like one idea or one action, logically leads to the next.

It's easy to expect that if you do this, then suddenly you'll find yourself ending with an answer.

Usually, what happens, is you end up in circles.

Welcome to a beautiful set of drawings, accompanied by a wonderful set of reflections that will help you see your career and decisions differently.

I love the ideas in this book, and the way Naishadh has created visual analogies to help us gain greater insight into sticky career, self-care, and job search situations.

He's shown us that great ideas and actions can co-exist side by side, that we don't need to consider one thing before we look at another.

He's given us ah-ha moments and he's pointed out some big home truths.

So how to use this book?

My suggestion is to pick a few pictures out that really resonate with you and keep them pinned up where you can see them for inspiration.

We process images far faster than words, so if you're looking for and quick clarity or an instant pick me up, it will be right there in front of you.

And do make sure you read the accompanying reflections from career experts all over the world and enjoy the insights and wisdom that are jammed packed inside.

The world needs more creative career books like this.

Thank you, Naishadh, for making it happen.

Karalyn Brown
Founder: Straight to Shortlist Challenge.

An Open Letter to Career Practitioners.

So, why would you look at a book full of career doodles?

Well, I think as career practitioners, we're too devoted to words.

We can often think what we say, and when and how we say it, will be enough to illustrate our ideas and inspire our clients into taking great action.

Yet actions are driven by emotions, which are hard to find the precise words for.

I am honoured that Naishadh asked me to write a forward for this book.

From the very first day that he started to share his daily doodles on LinkedIn, he has inspired career practitioners from around the world like me to see, feel and therefore think differently.

And he has done this with simple, yet evocative sketches.

But not only that, with his daily drawings, he's shown us that it's OK to do things differently.

In our own ways, we all help people uncover their unique strengths and encourage them to express these openly. But often as career practitioners, we're not great at doing this ourselves.

With this book and his social media sharing, Naishadh has raised the bar for us all to experiment with ideas, to share, to communicate, to openly be more creative – and to powerfully embody the messages we give clients.

And with that he's building a movement – a tribe of fans that spans the continents, which I am sure will keep snowballing to bigger things for all of us.

So, whether you're an experienced career practitioner or simply interested in visual ways of thinking, I do hope you find something to inspire you – and your own creative way to express this in your life.

Karalyn Brown
Founder: Straight to Shortlist Challenge.

Contents

Social Media/Personal Branding

Self-Development

Preface

"*Mr. Gadani, I don't believe you can learn how to draw,*" said Mr. Bhatia, my teacher at a technical school in a small town in western India, when he caught me peeking into my best friend's book. I felt embarrassed, but it didn't stop me from peeking again!

At that moment, I believed him. Drawing wasn't for me. I completed engineering, copying most of my engineering drawing assignments from a friend. It further fostered my belief. In the coming years, I never needed to use my drawing skills. However, I always considered myself creative and innovative.

During university, I became an avid reader of business magazines. I found them fascinating and inspiring. I invariably applied those learnings in my work but added masala (a spice blend!) to it. It was my X-factor, my stamp all over it. I really enjoyed the process of coming up with different ideas and communicating the message with simplicity.

Fast forward a few years, I arrived in Australia in 2007, and after a couple of redundancies in engineering roles, I changed my career and became an employment consultant. Working in the careers and employment sector opened my eyes, widened my horizons, expanded my understanding of the world of work, and gave me an opportunity to do some meaningful and impactful work.

It's not that I liked my work every day and jumped out of bed on Monday morning, but I knew that I had arrived home. This was me!

One of the important aspects of career practitioners' work is to interpret and apply career theories, models, and frameworks to clients' situations. It is not always easy. I have explained the hidden job market nearly a million times, and after a while, it becomes exhausting. I am sure my fellow career practitioner colleagues would agree with this sentiment.
I only realised that my learning preference is Visual, Kinaesthetic, Reading and

Writing and then Auditory. Let me tell you, if I knew this when I was at university, my career trajectory would have been completely different. Newspaper and print ads still make me curious. I am attracted to the simplicity of the message through visuals, use of colours, size of the fonts, and the drama it creates.

Now, I know you're asking, ***"Naishadh, come to the point buddy. No one's interested in your life story. We read this every day on LinkedIn!"*** Don't worry, I am getting close to the reason behind this book.

COVID shut the whole world down. Working from home meant I had time to pursue other things. That's when I decided to learn doodling. I completed an introductory course and enjoyed the process. Doodling gave me the freedom to be not precise. Doodling or sketching is a communication medium. I started experimenting as part of the LinkedIn Live show promotions. People loved it – at least they told me so!

It took another six months for me to start drawing metaphors to explain concepts. My first proper doodle was the Job Search Paradox. It explains the paradox of how job seekers look for jobs and how employers look for talent. I have used it multiple times in my coaching, and it works like magic. People get it! And I don't need to feel overwhelmed.

I think it was in June 2022 when Amanda McCue, an amazing Career Practitioner, commented on my post, ***"Naishadh, why don't you make these doodles available in a resource?"***.

It was an a-ha moment.

Wow! Can I do it?

I had always dreamed of being an author, so I decided to give it a try. However, I wanted to approach the book in a different way, so I came up with the idea of collaborating with people who had engaged with my doodles on LinkedIn.

They would write content based on my doodles, whether it was an anecdote, a story, a process, or a reflection.

It was a crazy idea, but I mustered the courage to reach out to career practitioners, coaches, entrepreneurs, and accomplished professionals across the world. I was overwhelmed by their positive response, and 46 amazing people agreed to be a part of the project.

Over the following weeks and months, I continued to draw doodles while they wrote about them. This book truly has been a global collaborative effort, and I'm deeply proud of it.

I would like to thank my long-time friend and collaborator Karalyn Brown for coming up with the book's name.

Also thank you to Meenakshi Iyer for suggesting "visual" word to be included in the tagline.

I'm also grateful to the following people who contributed to the book: Adele Chee, Alana Lane, Alex Barritt, Allan Gatenby, Dr Anamika Sharma, Amit Khanna, Andrew Perry, Bernie McFarlane, Brian Klindworth, Chris Webb, Chrissy De Blasis, Claire Harvey, Daniel Solodky, Dipti Pandit, Frank Interrigi, Freda Zapsalis, Gauri Gokhale, Heidi Winney, Helen Green, Jalpa Bhavsar, Jasmine Malki, Jennifer Barfield, Jenny Hale, Karen Thompson, Katherine Jennick, Kathryn Jackson, Karalyn Brown, Leigh Pickstone, Lis McGuire, Lynne Strong, Meenakshi Iyer, Melita Long, Natalie Sims, Nicola Barnard, Nicola Semple, Roohi Ahmad, Sally-Ann Monger, Sangeeta Mulchandani, Sarah Fogarty, Sarita Bahl, Serena Low, Sharon Kilmartin, Shrivi Aiyer, Susan Smith, Sushma Nagaraj, Suzi Chen, Utsav Gupta, Vaidehi Kavthekar, Vineti Anand's, and ChatGPT.

I am grateful to Marian Brown (Karalyn Brown's Mom) and Fiona Harvey (Claire Harvey's Mom) for proofreading the book.

I think the best way to approach this book is to let it inspire you. Flip through the pages and see what catches your eye. Perhaps it's a funny little sketch that makes you smile or a thought-provoking concept that sparks your imagination.

Whatever it is, I hope it motivates you to think outside the box and inspires you to act towards your career goals.

The BIG Book of Career Doodles is more than just a collection of sketches and stories; it's a reminder that your career journey is unique and that you have the power to shape it into something that truly makes you happy. Don't be afraid to take risks, to try something new, or to make mistakes. It's all part of the process, and each step you take brings you one step closer to the career you've always wanted.

In conclusion, I would like to thank everyone who has been a part of this book, whether as a contributor, supporter, or reader. I hope it brings a smile to your face, inspires you to think differently, and helps you on your journey towards a fulfilling and satisfying career.

Happy reading and possibly doodling!
Naishadh Gadani

www.thebigbookofcareersdoodles.com

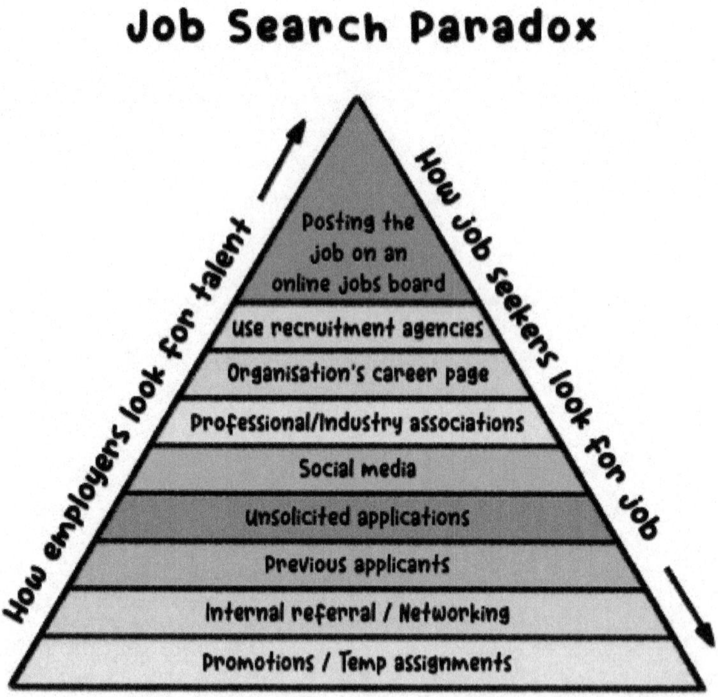
Job Search Paradox
Posting the job on an online jobs board
Use recruitment agencies
Organisation's career page
Professional/Industry associations
Social media
Unsolicited applications
Previous applicants
Internal referral / Networking
Promotions / Temp assignments
How employers look for talent
How Job seekers look for Job

Job Search Paradox

When employers begin looking for prospective candidates, they look for people who are known to them or have, in some way, proved that they are suitable for the role. This is a proactive approach that begins by looking closer to home, taking the line of least resistance. It is safer and easier for the employer to follow the path that requires the least effort and cost.

Familiarity, when it comes to employment, does not, in fact, breed contempt.

The job search paradox is that employers begin their recruitment drives from sources where candidates are most known to them, whereas job seekers begin at the point where employees are least known to them. The ends are, in fact, polar opposites. It stands to reason then that the further you can accommodate an employer's needs and communicate directly with them, the more successful you will be in securing employment.

Employers would prefer to hire people who are known to them or who have proactively approached them. In stark contrast, job seekers stick to their lane and respond passively to online adverts, not realizing it's the employer's last resort.

Job seekers need to be more proactive and begin conversations with recruiters, connect with employers, take part in work experience, insight weeks, or ask for informational interviews to get past being unknown and become known. Use focused time and meaningful connections in a proactive way as your job search tools instead of sitting back and only reacting to job adverts.

Proactive + Proactive = Result.

The next time you need to move jobs, think of employers like electricity; they take the line of least resistance, and if they encounter you on their path and you are known to them, then all the better!

Written By

Susan Smith RCDP, PHEA,
Founder of 'All Things Careers'. Moving clients from lost and lethargic to focused and fired up by giving them the tools to grant their work wishes & the careers to change their lives.

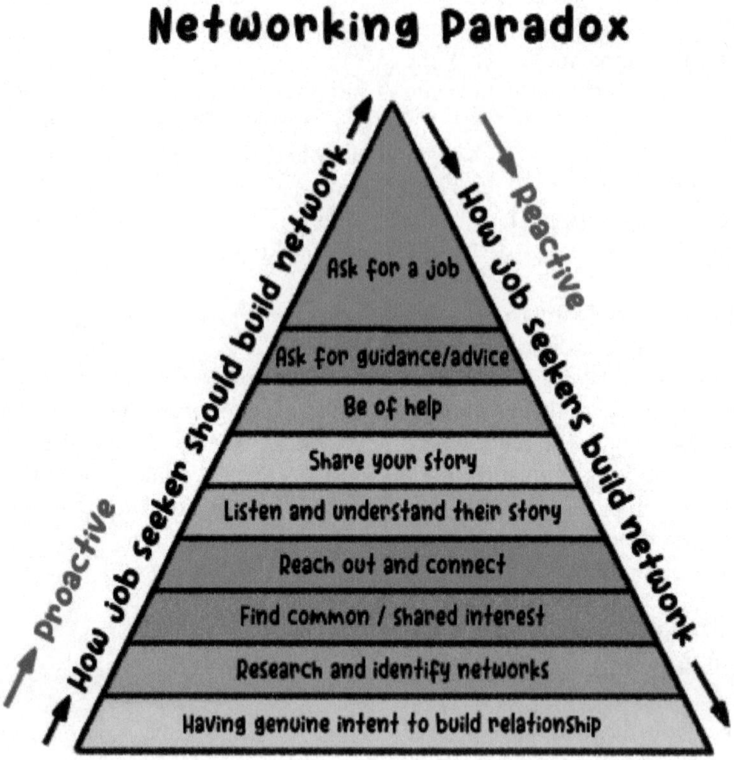
Networking Paradox
Ask for a job
Ask for guidance/advice
Be of help
Share your story
Listen and understand their story
Reach out and connect
Find common / shared interest
Research and identify networks
Having genuine intent to build relationship
Proactive
How job seeker should build network
Reactive
How job seekers build network

Networking Paradox

I have a confession: I HATE 'NETWORKING'. Now, this might sound like an odd admission given the image above, but please hear me out! You see, it's not the practice of networking that irks me, but rather the imagery that the word itself conjures in the minds of many people. In my experience working with students, graduates, and career changers, few words provoke a reaction like 'Networking.' For some, it is the anxiety linked to the thought of having to walk into a room of strangers and start striking up a conversation, while for others, it is the idea of forming a transactional relationship where the key focus is thinking 'what can this person do for me?' that puts them off.

And this is where the Networking Paradox comes in.

For so often, we not only approach but also understand networking the wrong way round, starting with the outcome and only worrying about the why afterwards. As the doodle above powerfully demonstrates, many job seekers approach networking as a means to an end (e.g., 'I'll connect with someone and see if they have any jobs going'), focusing on what they might be able to gain from this fleeting interaction rather than considering if it could develop into something even better. Now, this is an absolutely understandable approach, particularly for time-poor job seekers, but it is always going to be reactive in nature (e.g., I need something, I use networking to get it) and ensure that individuals miss out on the most valuable part of networking: building a community of supporters and advocates for yourself.

As the above doodle illustrates, when we approach the idea of networking from a more organic standpoint - for example, planning to connect with someone else purely on the basis of wanting to build a professional relationship with them - this naturally leads us to undertake a range of actions that are also beneficial for our own career development, such as researching industries/sectors of interest and joining relevant community groups to find out more about the things we might want to discuss with the person we are hoping to connect with. These actions not only move us closer to connecting with the individual we are interested in speaking with in a more authentic way (e.g., from a position of common interest), which naturally makes it more likely for someone to engage with us, but they also help us establish a routine for 'networking' that is more natural and less forced, smoothing the path for similar activity in the future.

This more proactive approach to networking not only maximizes our chances of establishing a community of individuals who genuinely want to help and support us, but it also gives us the opportunity to be exactly the same thing for someone else's network, now or in the future - we all need support from time to time within our careers and, when undertaken with reciprocal intent, networking offers us the chance to create communities that can enrich our professional lives in many different ways.

How do you build a network? Write your reflections.

Written By

Chris Webb
Registered Career Development Professional (RCDP), freelance careers writer/podcaster and co-host of the CDI's #WeAreCareers show.

What Can You Control in a Job Search?

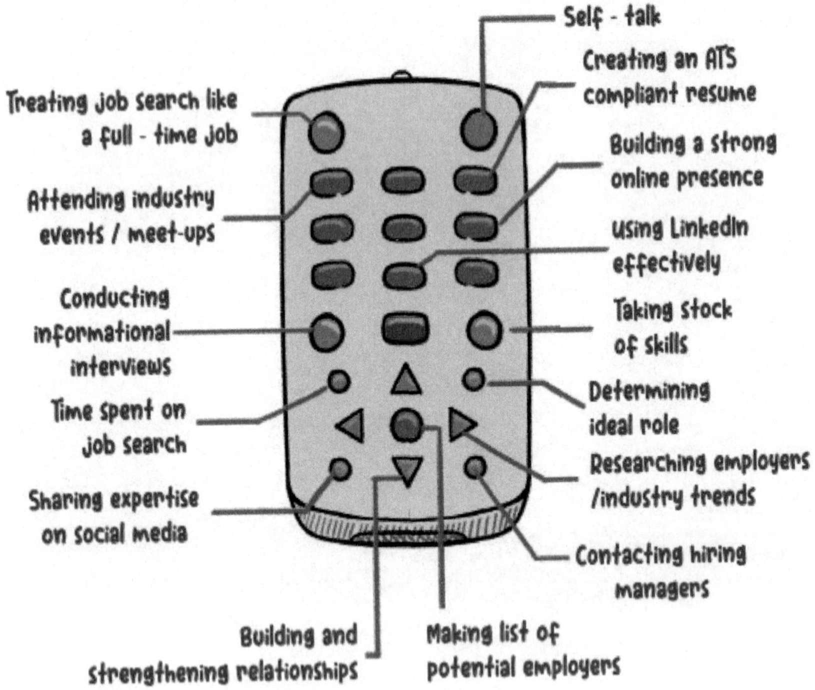

What Can You Control in a Job Search?

Often in the job search process, anxiety is experienced by worrying about things out of our control. By imagining a remote control of aspects you do have some control over, it may allow you to let go of worrying about those things you have no control over. When you think 'I don't know what to do', consider what other button you can press. Or if things aren't moving quickly enough, think 'what do I need to do more of?' and press some of the buttons again or more regularly.

Control button explanations:

- **Treating job search like a full-time job:** This is the ON button for your controller. By pressing (committing to) this, you are actively taking control of your activities and agreeing to get into action.
- **Completing skills assessment:** This can be pressed once each time the controller is turned on (each time you are looking to position yourself for a new job) to confirm and collate your value offering. It can also help you highlight what you may be missing that is required for a specific job.
- **Conducting informational interviews:** This is pressed to gain additional information to answer any questions you have about role types, skills and experience requirements, organisation culture, career journeys, interview and hiring processes. This button is used repeatedly and regularly throughout the job search process.
- **Self-talk:** This is something you can press to bring up subtitles for any of the dialogue going on in your head for any of the other button activities. This will ensure you are not missing any insight your subconscious is providing or to highlight any self-sabotaging thoughts that you may need to address objectively.
- **Attending industry events/ meet-ups:** This activity is to be done regularly at the start of the job search journey to gather information and grow your visibility. You may not see an instant reaction or return on investment of this activity, but be assured that it will add value when other buttons are pressed. So do it periodically.
- **Creating an ATS compliant resume:** You may only need to do this once each time the controller is activated, but it will need to be done for each type of role applying for. Other buttons will enhance this.
- **Building a strong online presence:** Pressing this regularly and targeted to your industry/ role focus will enhance the effectiveness of other buttons.

- **Using LinkedIn effectively:** This can be pressed once to update your profile at the beginning of a new job search. Then double-click regularly and multiple times (daily to weekly) to increase your visibility and network connections.
- **Time:** Press to allocate time for job search activities. This will minimize job search activity distractions during work, rest, and social times.
- **Determining your ideal role:** This is pressed when the controller is turned on but may be repressed to confirm or modify role focus if in long-term job search mode.
- **Sharing expertise on social media:** This can be pressed repeatedly throughout the job search process to increase visibility and show expertise to a wider audience but ideally operates in the background even when the job search controller is not activated.
- **Contacting hiring managers:** This is pressed after the 'Making list of potential employers' button and can be pressed periodically to keep in touch with company activities and industry trends.
- **Making a list of potential employers:** This provides a shortlist of organisations to research and people to connect with.
- **Researching employers:** In research mode, you will gather detailed information on each employer to determine role and culture fit.
- **Building relationships with recruiters:** Press when you have determined the role fit and type of organisation you want to work for. Only press if you have prior experience in the role you wish to apply for. Do not expect an immediate response, but this can be pressed periodically if you find a recruiter that services your industry or role type.

Written By

Nicola Barnard
Over 10 years of Career Development Consulting, assisting adults across a wide range of roles and industries to communicate their value.

What can you add to this list?

How do you remain in-charge of job search?

Job Search Bingo

I know the Job i am looking for	I know my career story	I know the impact I have made and can make	I have got the list of the potential employers who can hire me	I know the business problems I solve
I have developed a great resume	I have a proactive networking plan	I mix and match job search activities	I have prepared an elevator pitch	I only apply to relevant jobs
I got a great team of cheerleaders around me	I have not stopped pursuing my hobby	I am becoming effective on LinkedIn	I am building a great online presence	I attend face-to-face and online networking events
I create and post relevant content on LinkedIn	I attempt to help other job seekers	I proactively build recruiter relationships	I remain optimistic about my future	I reach out to hiring managers directly
I have a mentor who helps during this journey	I follow-up on all the applications	I love what I do	I am employing creative approaches to find job	I am proud of my career journey

Job Search Bingo

Looking for a job can be a challenging and time-consuming task, especially if you're not sure where to start or how to go about it. The Job Search Bingo is a fun way to work out a strategy while emphasizing key factors like self-awareness, timely preparation, a human-centric approach, support systems, and reflection.

Self-awareness is the first key factor highlighted in the Job Search Bingo. Being aware of your position in the career path and the current job market can help you streamline your job search strategy and determine the necessary steps to attain your objectives. This is an essential step because better awareness helps you target your efforts towards valuable career pathways.

The second key factor is timely preparation that should come long before the actual job application. Putting together a great resume, elevator pitch, job search platforms, and having a networking plan ready can help you prepare for the job search. Timely preparation also requires timely review without going down the hole of perfectionism, testing out the elevator pitch, and revising it to a stage that works in most scenarios. In my experience while working in higher education space, international students who are diligent with preparation tend to succeed much better!

A human-centric approach can be the key to capturing that ideal role (seen in multiple rows). Despite many job platforms and advertised jobs in the market, many job seekers struggle to succeed in the application process, which indicates a mismatch between employer expectations and what candidates are willing to offer. In my experience as a recruiter, hiring managers are always conscious of hiring someone for their team. That's why it can be beneficial to reach out to hiring managers and understand their expectations beyond the words mentioned in the position description.

The fourth key factor is support systems that can be an X factor in someone's career progression. Having a healthy, continuous relationship with a mentor or recruiter can open doors beyond imagination. And support systems can be availed of in the form of technology too! Think about LinkedIn, ChatGPT, resume review websites, etc.

And the last factor is reflection, which is highly underrated in my opinion. Reflection leads to continuous improvement in job applications, overcoming unexpected hurdles, and most importantly, keeps our mental health in check! By reflecting on your job search process, you can identify areas that need improvement and take steps to address them. It helps in keeping the motivation alive and focusing on your long-term goals.

In conclusion, the Job Search Bingo doodle is an informative yet fun way to navigate the job search process. By checking the relevant boxes and keeping the above-mentioned key factors in mind, one can increase their chances of finding the right job.

How many bingo boxes do you tick?

Written By

Utsav Gupta
Enabling meaningful, sustainable & inclusive careers.
Advisor - Careers & Employability
The University of Queensland.

Resume Bingo

My resume starts with a profile section	My resume has accomplishment stories relevant to the job	My resume flows logically	My resume does not go too far in experience	My resume highlights relevant experience
My resume has skills section	My resume has adequate white space	My resume doesn't look cluttered	My resume is easy to understand in my absence	I have embedded powerful action verbs
I have not used lot of colors	My resume doesn't have my picture	My resume is formatted professionally	I have not repeated same responsibilities	My resume is free of typos and grammatically accurate
I have included social media links	My resume doesn't include references	I have explained employment gaps	My resume doesn't have unsubstantiated claims of greatness	My resume's headings are clear
I always tailor resume for every application	I have created an awesome resume	I have included best practices in resume development	My resume has consistent employment period YY-YY or M/YY - M/YY	My resume captures readers' interest

Resume Writing: the Journey Over the Outcome

"Writing my own resume has been one of the most dreadful, soul sucking jobs I have ever had to do" - Anonymous Student, 2021.

I have found, as a secondary school teacher who has also worked as a quasi-career development practitioner in schools, that students are typically wholly focused on the end-product of a resume and often believe that they have little to no experience to draw on to create a good one. Afterall, most are applying for their first job so what work experience could they possibly draw on to get their first job (always a fun paradox to open the first lesson with)? Whilst we eventually go on to explore the roles of transferable skills, volunteer work, micro-credentials, hobbies and the like to address this, the richness of the resume development process is often lost to the focus of just getting the resume done.Despite the efforts of this early career teacher who wanted her students to see the value of the process through an accessible constructivist career counselling lens (Brown & Lent, 2013; Savickas, 2019; Savickas & Hartung, 2012; Scholl &Cascone, 2010).

Scholl and Cascone (2010) outline their beliefs "...that the constructivist resume career counselling approach, which includes a four-session model, can assist students in developing a clearer, more complex sense of their professional identity as well as increase their levels of career adaptability.... incorporate elements, including goal development and action planning..." (p. 183). In short, a constructivist resume includes past and present achievements and activities just like a traditional resume, however, it also presents desired and/or anticipated achievements and activities 5 to 7 years ahead. Whilst not submittable to an employer, the process of creating a constructivist resume can provide direction and focus for a student's learning as they look towards their future, what and who they may want to become and begin to lay the foundations for their imagined future.

From the perspective of a secondary teacher, resume bingo presents as a useful tool for students that gamifies the process of traditional resume development. As an individual, students can construct their resume and call out bingo when they have completed the necessary tasks. Alternatively, as part of a whole class activity, once all students have finished their first drafts, the entire class participates in a round of resume bingo as a means of conducting a final check. Another thought is that perhaps it can be expanded to incorporate elements found within less traditional resumes, such as the constructivist resume.

References

Brown, S. D., & Lent, R. W. (2013). Career development and counseling : Putting theory and research to work
(2nd ed.). Wiley.

Savickas, M. (2019). Career construction counseling manual. Mark L. Savickas. Savickas, M., & Hartung, P. (2012). My Career Story: An Autobiographical Workbook for Life-Career Success. Vocopher. http://www.vocopher.com/CSI/CCI_workbook.pdf

Scholl, M. B., &Cascone, J. (2010). The Constructivist Résumé: Promoting the Career Adaptability of Graduate Students in Counseling Programs The Career Development Quarterly, 59(2), 180–191. https://doi.org/10.1002/j.2161-0045.2010.tb00061.x

Written By

Sarah Marie Fogarty
PhD Candidate @ Edith Cowan University I apply multidisciplinary experience, creative systems thinking and research skills to navigate challenges the education sector.

Review your resume and check how many boxes do you tick ?

Job Search Shake
Recruiter relationship
Social media
Informational interviews
Approaching employers
Networking
Online application
Try until you like the taste

Job Search Shake

Over the years, I've spoken to a lot of frustrated job seekers. *"I've applied for so many roles without success,"* they say.

When I probe deeper, I discover that the only tool they have used has been online submissions for job advertisements they have seen. It's true, some people get a job this way, but there are many more options open to you, and the best approach is a combination of methods. Let's call it 'a blended approach.'

Much of my career has been spent in the recruitment industry. Career-smart people understand the importance of building a great relationship with a specialist recruiter in their field, even if they aren't looking to change roles in the immediate future. Top recruiters know what is happening in the industries they work with. They know of opportunities before they hit the open market. By developing a strong relationship with a good recruiter, you will be top of mind when the right role becomes available.

Career-smart people also understand the importance of building a great network. How is your network looking? Through your relationships with colleagues, industry associates, university alumni, friends, and family, you can connect with a multitude of people across the globe.

If you are looking to work in a particular field, ask those in your network who they may know that could help. This isn't about asking outright for a job but is a great way to arrange an informational interview. These are conversations with people who work in a particular industry or organisation, in which you can ask about their role or their career journey. Not only does this expand your knowledge and network, but it also places you at the forefront of their mind should an opening arise at their workplace.

The advent of social media has enabled us to open so many doors that were once firmly closed. Having a LinkedIn profile and understanding how best to use this platform to interact with others is essential for job seekers today. You can connect with fellow professionals, research organisations, and showcase your skills and expertise, potentially attracting recruiters to you. It also gives you an 'in' to approach organisations directly. In the past, it may have been a case of going door-to-door with your resume. Now, through online communication, you can build connections and have conversations that may lead to employment opportunities.

If you're looking for a new role, now or in the future, be career-smart and start adding ingredients to your blender today to create a delicious job search success shake. Good luck!

How do you like your Job Search Shake?

Written By

Karen Thompson
founder of Communicate U is a marketer, educator and recruitment specialist who helps YOU Communicate YOU!

What else can you add or remove to make your Job Search Shake?

8 Video Interview Hacks

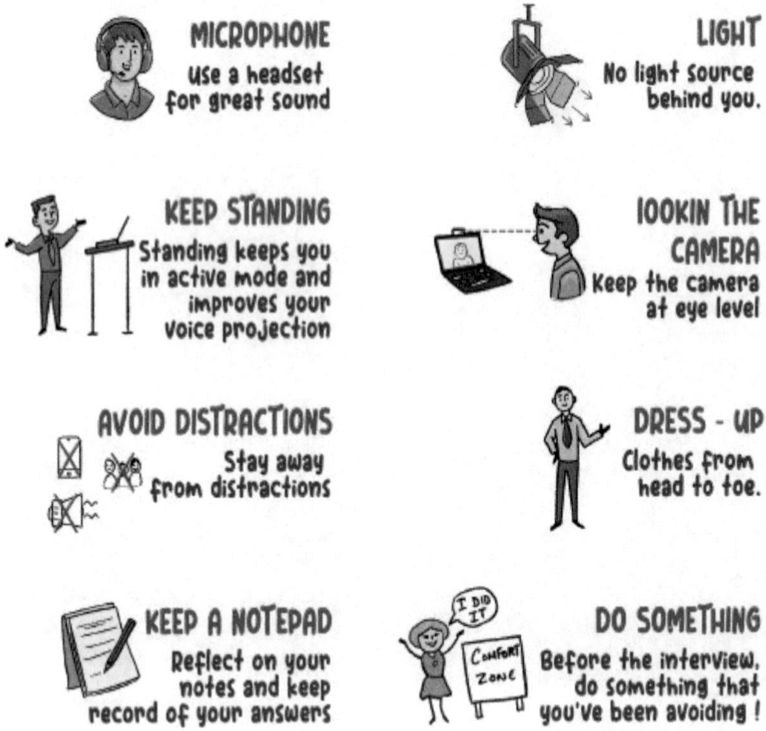
MICROPHONE
Use a headset for great sound
LIGHT
No light source behind you.
KEEP STANDING
Standing keeps you in active mode and improves your voice projection
lOOKIN THE CAMERA
Keep the camera at eye level
AVOID DISTRACTIONS
Stay away from distractions
DRESS - UP
Clothes from head to toe.
KEEP A NOTEPAD
Reflect on your notes and keep record of your answers
I DID IT
COMFORT ZONE
DO SOMETHING
Before the interview, do something that you've been avoiding !

8 Tips to Ace Your Next Video Interview

Following these practical steps can help you feel more comfortable and present at your best:

1. **Microphone:** Use an effective microphone to be heard without background noise and invest in a good webcam ideally with 1080 pixels. Ensure your face is large in the centre of the screen, with headroom above you and your shoulders visible.
2. **Light:** Position yourself facing a window, or the webcam will expose for the light, and you won't be seen. Ensure that ceiling lights aren't visible. You can use a standing desk. Ensure the wall behind you is blank or very tidy. If you are in a dark room, add extra lights to shine more light on your face.
3. **Keep Standing:** A good reason to use a standing desk. Like presenting to an audience, it's more effective standing up. It helps you have better posture, breathe better, project your voice effectively and appear more confident.
4. **Look in the camera:** If you are talking to one interviewer put them on Presenter mode and focus on them. If you have more than one interviewer, use Gallery mode and look at the person who asked you the question when responding, same as a face-to-face interview. It's ok to have notes of what you want to say. Tack them in sticky notes onto a wall behind your screen.
5. **Avoid distractions:** In a virtual interview, you need to proactively reduce your distractions. Have your interview in a closed room or send your family members away so they don't disturb you. The biggest distractions come from devices, so turn off every other app, silence all notifications, and turn off your phone.
6. **Dress-up:** Don't risk getting busted, dress up properly for an interview. If in doubt, always dress up, not down, and wear a suit. It creates a better impression, puts you in interview mode, and improves how you come across. Try it, and you'll see what I mean.
7. **Keep a notepad:** Reflect on your notes and keep a record of your answers: Pre- prepare your written interview answers or mind map of achievement stories, based on likely job-based interview questions, and keep them handy. You are less likely to forget, which gives you confidence. Use a notepad to note questions, role/company information, and your own reflections.

8. **Do something before the interview:** Here are things you can do to help get yourself into a positive mindset.

A. Ask your friends and loved ones to remind you what they admire about you and what you are good at. This will help boost your confidence.

B. Practice deep breathing into your belly for 2 minutes. This will reduce your heart rate by up to 20 BPM, calm nerves, dampen your fight/flight response, and help you think clearly.

C. Stand in the superhero pose, legs apart and hands on your hips for 2 minutes before your interview. Amy Cuddy's research shows this will boost your confidence and lower stress.

What has worked for you in a video interview?

Written By

Melita Long, Careers on Purpose
Career & Executive Coach, LinkedIn & Resume Writer, 20 years helping mid-career professionals identify and achieve their ideal career.

When looking for a job,
actions speak louder than thinking!

Bias Towards Action

If a picture is worth a thousand words, then considered action is worth a thousand thoughts. When careful thoughts meet action, magic happens.

There are many reasons why we often end up overthinking when job hunting. A drawn-out application process, feeling rejected, feeling like an imposter, unsure about what to do, unfavourable visa restrictions, the list of reasons can go on.

Irrespective of their validity, the result is that these reasons turn us into procrastinators, preventing us from moving forward. The only antidote available in this case is taking action.

I am a strong advocate of taking considered action for two reasons. Firstly, in an ever-evolving job market, whoever second-guesses themselves into inaction often ends up going backwards.

"Backwards? But how?"

Well, if everyone else has moved forward, then whoever stays in the same place is actually going backwards, relatively speaking.

Secondly, the biggest benefit of taking considered action is the opportunity to reshape our environment and make it more favourable for us to succeed in the long term. And I have just the perfect story to share on this point.

Years ago, a mentee of mine who was an international student was struggling to find a full-time position in his chosen field. He was a strong candidate if it wasn't for the fact that he was on an international student visa.

After many hours spent ruminating over the visa limitation, he realised he needed to improve his chances through tangible action. Interestingly, he decided on a traditional approach to reshaping his environment.

Armed with several physical copies of his resume, he walked the streets, knocked on the door of the companies that he wished to join, and asked to speak to the HR manager in person.

It wasn't easy, but his dedication made an impression. The hard work paid off. My mentee was offered a position by one of the companies that he visited and he has since gone from strength to strength, taking on other opportunities to further his career in Australia.

This example shows that, by taking considered action, one could reshape their environment and tip the balance gradually in their favour. But of course, tipping the balance takes time. That's why taking consistent action and making small but steady progress is the key.

Remember, considered action is worth a thousand thoughts.

In which areas of your career have you been considering taking action, but have not done so? What has been the impact of not taking action? Additionally, what specific actions are you currently taking to move forward?

Written By

Dr Suzi Chen
Self-Leadership Advocate, Impact Investor & Founder @ Notonos & Resilient Leadership Academy Developing resilient leaders with purposeful career through self-leadership.

Two Ways to Get the Job You Deserve

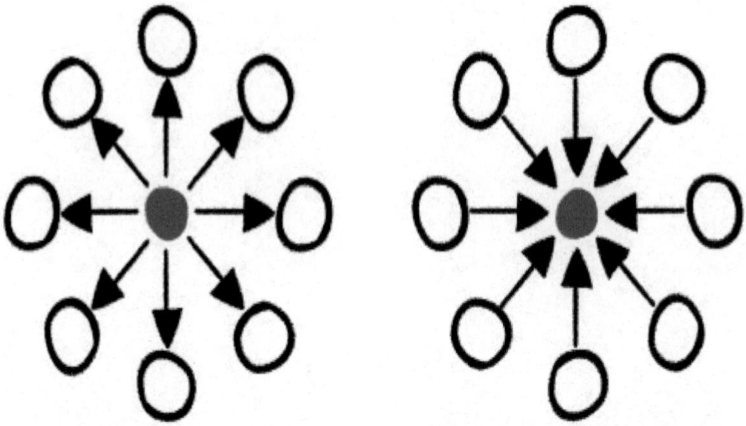

Apply for jobs.
Chase employers.

Attract employers.
Build a personal brand.

Two Ways to Find Work

While there are many ways to get the job you deserve, this doodle depicts two ways you can search for, identify and secure opportunities.

Reactive Job Search

The image on the left relates to adopting a reactive job search, meaning you look for work passively. This is a very popular job search method, with the majority of jobseekers only applying to positions they see advertised online on job boards, or on company websites. In essence, you 'chase employers' for opportunities.

The problem with a reactive job search is that you are often going up against hundreds of other applicants, so the competition is fierce. Another issue is that each year, on average, only 25% of available positions are formally advertised online. This means that the remaining 75% of positions are informally 'advertised' and filled via what is known as the 'hidden' job market.

Given this 'hidden' job market contains the majority of Australian jobs, jobseekers can no longer rely on formally advertised positions alone to find work. This is why adopting a proactive job search is so important.

Proactive Job Search

The image on the right relates to adopting a proactive job search. A proactive job search involves identifying and attracting opportunities before they are advertised, allowing you to tap into the hidden job market. One sure way to attract opportunities and employers is to develop a strong personal brand. Your personal brand tells others who you are, what unique skills, strengths, expertise and experiences you offer, and what your personal values include.

Your personal brand also communicates your value proposition, that is, a statement or summary detailing your skills, background or expertise that differentiates you from your competition. Your value proposition also demonstrates what makes you unique and why you're the best fit for a particular position or organisation.

Benefits of Personal Branding

When done effectively, your personal brand can help you build a strong reputation, leading to new opportunities, powerful connections and strong networks that enhance both your personal and professional life. Effective personal branding also elevates your online and market presence, allowing you to become more accessible and visible among prospective employers and recruiters.

So, instead of 'chasing employers', your personal brand will attract employers, leading to authentically engaged career conversations and opportunities.

If you are changing careers or entering / re-entering the workforce, focus on the skills, value and experiences that are transferrable and which meet the needs of the organisations or employers you are targeting.

What strategies have you used in your job search?

Written By

Chrissy De Blasis
Certified Career Practitioner & Director @ Career Revival. Dedicated to supporting individuals from all walks of life and all stages of their career journeys.

What has worked and what has not worked?

Job Search Snakes and Ladders

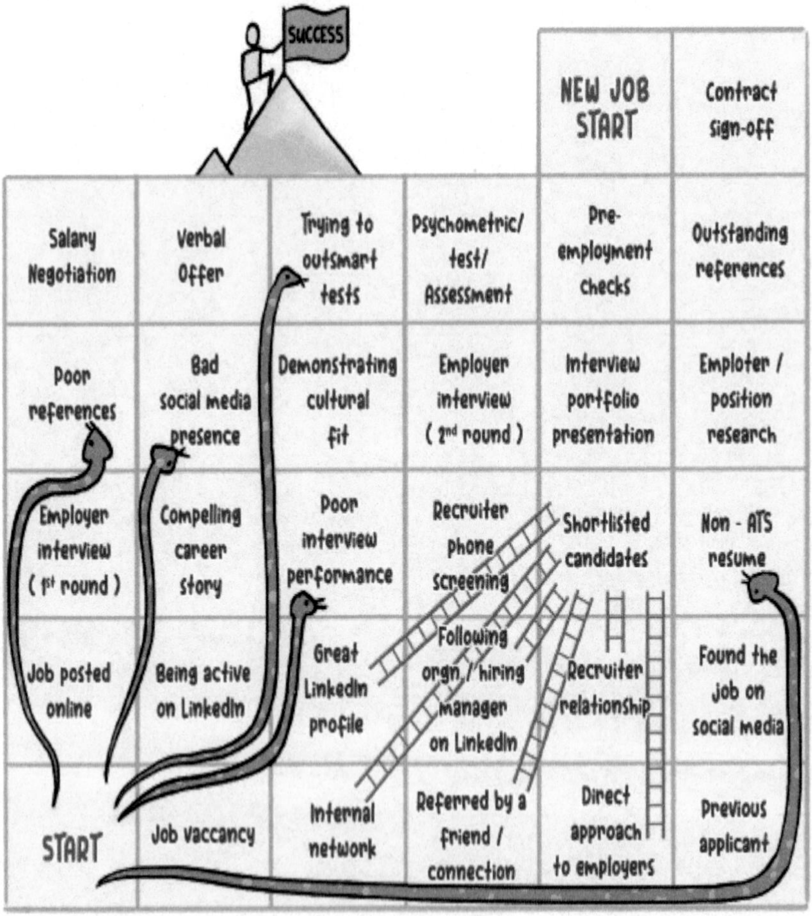

Job Search Snakes and Ladders

The world can be likened to a game of snakes and ladders, with different aspects of our lives mirroring this. This can also be represented by the opportunities we take or miss in our careers.

At times, you may get a ladder and move to a higher position, while at other times, you may obtain a snake and fall to a lower level. When you apply for jobs and go through the process of securing a position, it may feel like a game of snakes and ladders.

Although there are processes involved in job applications, this does not always guarantee the same process will be applied each time you apply for a role. Each organisation has its way of shortlisting and employing potential candidates for a vacant position. This could involve a face-to-face interview, video or phone call, technical tests, portfolio presentations, or a combination of these. You may have an idea of what to expect but not know precisely what is in store. Therefore, it is crucial to prepare for any outcome, implement strategies based on past experiences, and remain flexible so that you can get back into action even if you are unsuccessful in your application.

Not getting the position you applied for may feel like you are back to the beginning of the whole process, like a game of snakes and ladders. However, it is important to realise that you are merely back to the start of the board, not the game itself. You can make choices that could potentially affect the outcome, such as rolling the dice at an angle or spinning them instead. You can change the way you play the game based on your past experiences, and the same applies to job applications.

There will be times when you have put in all your effort and improved your actions and skillset based on past experiences, but you will not be shortlisted or successful. The reasons are countless; some may relate to your performance at the time, while others could result from the competition you are up against in securing the job. Chances are, you have done everything correctly, but the employer might find someone else who was more suited to the role. You may have rolled the dice really well to obtain high numbers every time, only to have a snake drag you down on a later roll. There is nothing wrong with the way you rolled the dice, but just sheer unluckiness on that turn.

We often forget that success will not always be immediate and can vary from person to person. Sometimes there are factors within our control, and others occur by chance.

Your experience will vary between each organisation and can influence your approach to searching and applying for jobs. Building from these experiences, you can incorporate strategies to increase your chances of success in each stage. However, understanding that the whole process and transition between each stage can be random, just like a game of snakes and ladders, is crucial.

What ladders have helped you in the job search process? Write your reflections.

Written By

Sushma Nagaraj
Passionate about working with diverse communities with a desire to create positive change in people's lives.

What snakes have damaged your job search process?

Cannonball and Networking

Cannonball and Networking

A cannon is a very old system used to propel grenades into enemy territory while keeping a safe distance.

The way it works is by harnessing the power of chemical reactions to propel the cannonball forward with full force.

Typically, a chemical reaction is a process where one or more substances (the reactants) are converted into a different product, meant for a different purpose. Simply put, a new substance is created by breaking down the molecules of an atom using a chemical reaction that is already present.

When a cannonball is lit and fired, a heat source starts a chemical reaction that rapidly converts a solid into a gas. This gas pushes the cannonball out, sending it flying towards its target, aiming to create a huge impact.

Networking is like that chemical reaction, creating a resultant force that provides a powerful impact in the world of connections, businesses or employment.

The territory may not be that of an enemy, but it is unknown and difficult to access.

Networking and referrals create an atmosphere that, like the created gas, pushes the applicant beyond the territorial and on-ground challenges, like going through very specialised application processes, getting picked up in recruitment apps, and receiving calls for interviews.

It then lands on the table, passing many unknown hurdles, and creates an environment where the pertinent people end up looking at and giving cognisance to your resume because of the people who threw it in their direction and because of its sheer velocity!

So, a connection created for a different purpose at a different time ends up becoming a different product, harnessing a different goal, such as a job offer!

Let me give an example from my life.

In 2005, the Department of Gandhian Studies at the University of Delhi, India, was desperately looking for a suitable candidate at the level of Assistant Professor. The main criterion was to have an academic to propagate Gandhian philosophy in different colleges, but that candidate should not

be from political studies departments because they wanted a fresh look at the deeper meanings of Gandhi's words and infuse them in education.

Regular advertisements and job boards presented only students of political studies, resulting in unsuccessful interviews.

On the other side of the spectrum was me, a scholar in Linguistics, specialising in Stylistics (studying styles of languages), looking for a job outside regular teaching positions.

Networking got me connected to a professor who knew another professor, who knew the Department of Gandhian Studies and their requirements, and the contact information was exchanged.

The rest is history.

How have you used networking in job search and career development?

Written By

Dr Anamika Sharma
Career Consultant and Linguist. An Agile and Life-long Learner.

What have you learnt about yourself in the process?

Job Search Self-Care Necklace
Celebrate small wins
Deliberate practice
Stay connected
Look after your physical health
Pursue hobby
Be clear about your next career goal
Establish and maintain daily routine
Take regular breaks
Reach-out / Ask for help and support
Focus on what you can control
Compassion
Keep and maintain perspective

Job Search Self-Care Necklace

Looking for a job can be a challenging and often stressful experience. It's easy to get caught up in the job search process and neglect our own self-care. That's where the Self-Care Necklace comes in - a metaphor for the different aspects of self-care that can help us stay focused, motivated, and energized during the job search process. Let's explore the 11 beads of the Self-Care Necklace and how they can support us during our job search journey.

1. **Celebrate small wins:** Job searching can often feel like an uphill battle, but it's important to celebrate every victory along the way. Whether it's getting an interview or receiving positive feedback, acknowledging and celebrating small wins can help boost our confidence and motivation.
2. **Stay connected:** Networking and building relationships are crucial components of a successful job search. Whether it's reaching out to former colleagues or attending industry events, staying connected to our professional network can provide us with valuable support, advice, and job leads.
3. **Look after your physical health:** Job searching can be mentally and emotionally draining, but it's important not to neglect our physical health. Eating well, getting enough sleep, and exercising regularly can help us stay energized, focused, and ready to tackle whatever challenges come our way.
4. **Establish and maintain a daily routine:** Maintaining a consistent daily routine can help us stay organized, focused, and productive during the job search process. This includes setting aside dedicated time for job searching, networking, and self-care activities.
5. **Reach out to others and ask for help:** Job searching can be overwhelming, and it's okay to ask for help. Whether it's reaching out to a mentor or seeking support from a career coach, asking for help can provide us with valuable guidance, perspective, and encouragement.
6. **Practice compassion:** Job searching can be a stressful and emotional process, and it's important to practice self-compassion along the way. This includes being kind to ourselves, recognizing our strengths, and acknowledging that setbacks and rejections are a normal part of the job search process.
7. **Keep and maintain perspective :** Job searching can be all-consuming, but it's important to maintain perspective and keep our long-term goals in mind. This includes recognizing that the job

search process is a journey and that setbacks and rejections are opportunities for growth and learning.

8. **Focus on what you can control:** Job searching can be unpredictable, but focusing on what we can control can help us stay grounded and focused. This includes identifying our strengths and skills, tailoring our job search strategies, and setting realistic goals and expectations.
9. **Take regular breaks:** Job searching can be a marathon, not a sprint. Taking regular breaks to recharge and refresh can help us stay motivated, focused, and avoid burnout. Whether it's taking a walk, meditating, or simply taking a few
10. **Be clear about your next goal :** Having a clear goal in mind can help us stay motivated and focused during the job search process. This includes setting specific, measurable, achievable, relevant, and time-bound (SMART) goals and creating a plan to achieve them. Having a clear goal can also help us prioritize our tasks and make better decisions about how to spend our time and resources.
11. **Pursue a hobby:** Job searching can be a stressful and all-consuming process, but it's important to maintain a healthy work-life balance. Pursuing a hobby or interest outside of the job search can help us relax, recharge, and develop new skills and interests. Whether it's taking up a new sport or joining a book club, pursuing a hobby can help us maintain perspective and find fulfillment outside of work.

In conclusion, the Self-Care Necklace is a powerful metaphor for the different aspects of self-care that are essential during the job search process

Credits: Originated with CHATGPT AI, polished by Naishadh Gadani

CHATGTP is property of OpenAI

Written By

Naishadh Gadani
Engineer turned Career Practitioner. Author. Doodler. Presenter. Non-TEDx Speaker. Helping people design their careers.

Write your reflections on the doodle.

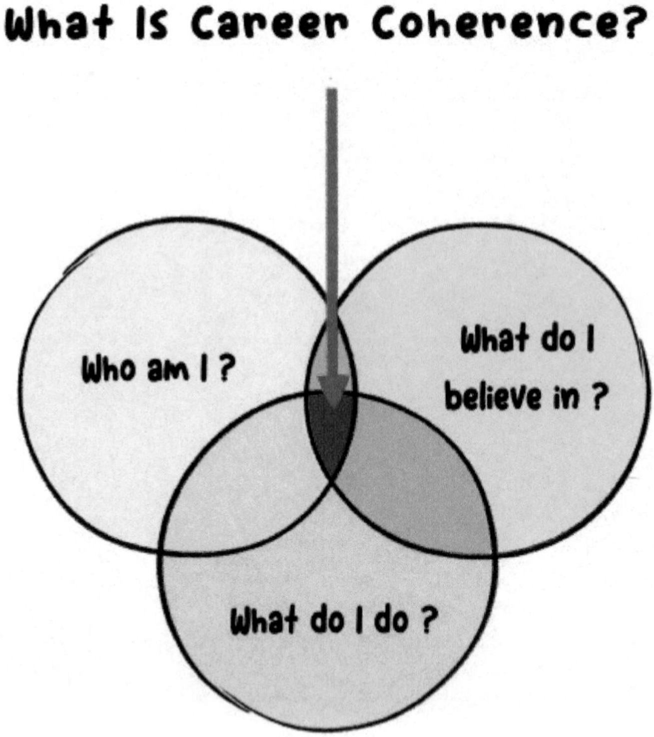
What Is Career Coherence?
Who am I ?
What do I believe in ?
What do I do ?

What Is Career Coherence?

Career coherence, in my view, is the holistic synergy that occurs when an individual has a strong sense of their self-identity and self-clarity across all pillars of their life. This has never been more important since the beginning of the pandemic, with the rapid acceleration and constant changes to the future of work, and the stress this has placed on individual's' sense of self and purpose in their career. How many people have felt, or are still feeling, like they are weathering the storm, waiting for the next set of pounding waves to hit, all the while questioning:

• Who am I? • What do I believe in? • What do I do?

In terms of self-clarity and career coherence, it is akin to building your house on the sand. It can collapse easily if you don't have self-clarity before you build your house Building material includes:

- Skills
- Interests
- Personality Types
- Values
- Education's where it is taking you

Self-reflection is key to gaining a strong sense of ourselves, especially these days when things are so busy, and many people are in transitions. Yet we often don't take time in an intentional way to engage in self-reflection about our career and how this is coherent to our sense of self, until situations change that force us to make career pivots.

With a real focus in our world right now on climate change, the environment, who we are in the world, self-reflection lets us put ourselves into the world in a bigger kind of way, leading us to a sense of mattering and Green Career thinking. Perhaps you might take time to ask yourself, "what am I doing that will make the world a better place?"

I have noticed this sense of loss of self-identity and purpose, for example, with some military personnel who have transitioned or are transitioning from the military to the civilian environment, along with changing culture, life roles, and work structure. Identifying and establishing career coherence, in my opinion, can go a long way in supporting and sustaining career transitions.

My biggest tip would be to give yourself permission to take time to reflect and explore these pondering questions above and try some of the strategies listed below.

Some strategies I have used myself and with clients during the process of finding purpose include:

- Allow your mind to wander and reflect on your situation and passions.

- Visualisation strategies for how you see your future. Where did you see yourself, for example, in five years? Who is there? What are you doing? How are you feeling, etc.?
- Identify and align your core values.
- Reflect upon those things in life about which you are passionate.
- Identify activities and experiences that give you joy.
- Make a mural/collage board of what/who makes your heart sing.
- List three skills that you enjoy using the most – it can be in your current role or a previous one.

Who am I?

Written By

Jennifer (Jenn) Barfield RPCDP, PCDAA, CHATP
Career Development Professional. Empowering people to sustain action-oriented hope. Specialises in Veteran and Military Spouse career journeys.

What do I believe in?

What do I do?

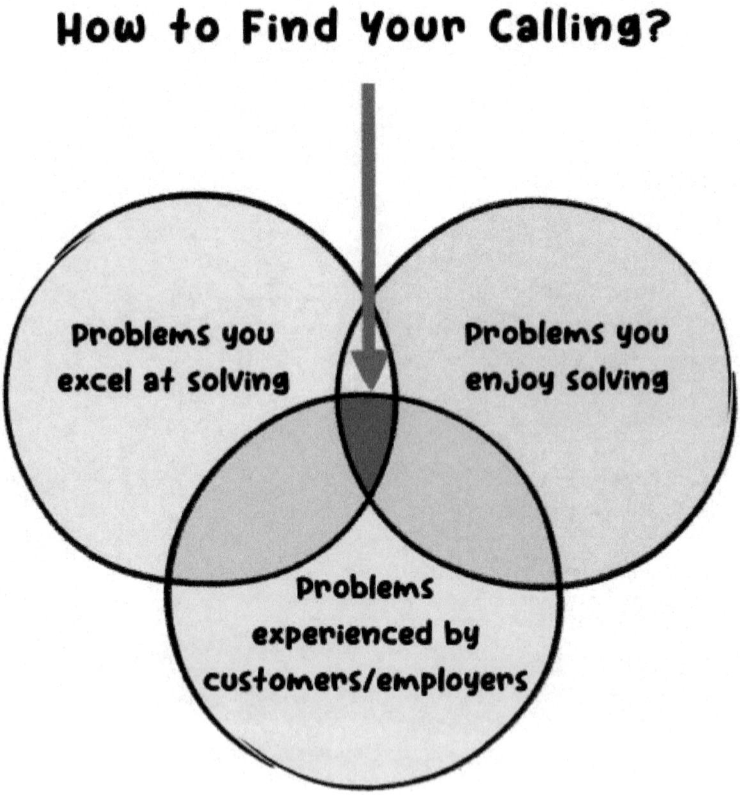
How to Find Your Calling?
Problems you excel at solving
Problems you enjoy solving
Problems experienced by customers/employers

How to Find Your Calling?

For all of us, the ringtone is different. It could be a silent vibration or a high volume BBBRRRRIIINNNGG.

So when trying to find or hear your 'calling," it can be helpful to break it down into three ways of thinking.

The first way of thinking is to consider the problems you are good at solving. Think about the skills and capabilities you have mastered. Skills are particular learned abilities we need to perform a job, duty, or task well. Competencies are our behaviors and knowledge which lead us to be successful in our tasks, duties, and jobs. Throughout our working lives, remember that we work in all aspects of our life, be it paid work, home/ life work, hobby work, or volunteer work. We develop capabilities and skills required and transferable to the workplace. What problems are you good at solving? Is there a particular task or role you are naturally drawn to or asked to contribute to?

The second way of thinking focuses on the problems you enjoy solving. This is not about mastery. It is about enjoyment; we can be very good at things and not enjoy them! You may be thinking about changing, pivoting, or retraining for future employment. This way of thinking can also be about growth and development. What do you find satisfaction in? What do you want to be able to do better? What problems do you find yourself volunteering to solve? When you are "working" at solving problems/ contributing/planning/committing to, what makes time fly? What gives you positive feedback, a sense of accomplishment or satisfaction?

The third way of thinking is focusing on the problem faced by employers or customers. This way of thinking relates to the job market. Labor market information can help us to understand who might employ people who solve problems they are good at or enjoy. Once you identify those problems you enjoy or are good at solving, you can use them to form part of your job search. For example, if you want to solve technical issues, fix, or repair things, you can use these terms in an online job search. The information generated can help to identify organisations or vacancies, roles unknown to us as job seekers. We can then create a network by researching and linking to these organisations to find out what projects and services purpose they have and who works there.

A helpful way of thinking about a job search is to think of it as a problem that needs solving. An organisation has a problem - a job vacancy - and is looking for someone to solve that problem - an employee. The more the job seeker knows enough about their skills, capabilities, and unique value, the more meaningful and successful the applications will be. Problem solved! Calling heard!

What problems do you excel at solving?

Written By

Natalie Sims - Career Tree - Grow Your Future
Career Development Professional - NEC CDANZ Delivering Free Career Guidance to All New Zealanders.

What problems do you like solving?

What problems are experienced by your customers/employers?

What Can You Control in Career Growth?

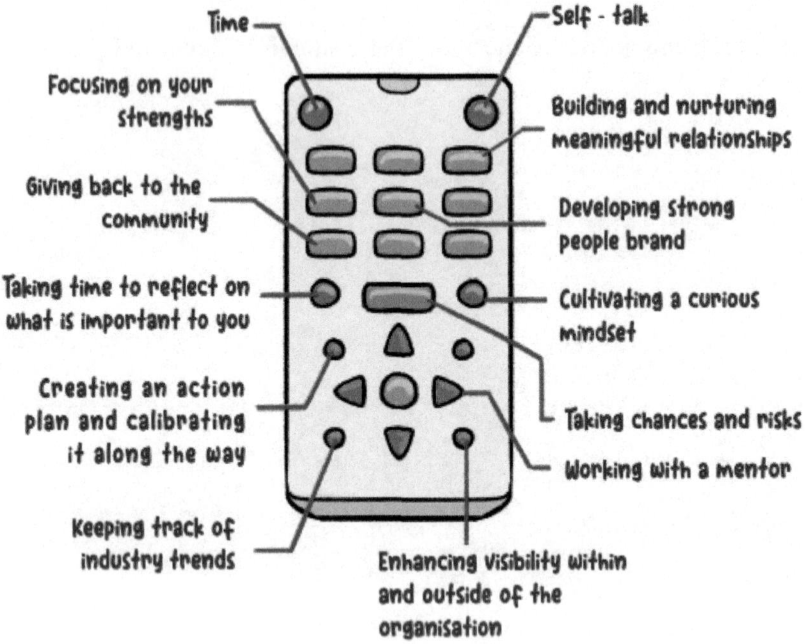

What Can You Control in Career Growth?

This doodle is packed full of fabulous advice, starting with the very idea of control. Focusing on things you cannot control can tip you off balance. You can get distracted worrying about what other people think, world crises, the economy, etc. It can suck the life out of you and leave you feeling anxious. A healthier, more productive approach is to focus on things you can control. This doodle gives lots of ideas for that. I am going to focus on the big one:

Building and nurturing meaningful relationships. This one is gold.

Zig Ziglar said, "You can get everything in life you want if you will just help enough other people get what they want".

That might seem counterintuitive. It is certainly counterculture! While it might go against your instinct, it is actually very true. If you are generous and open with other people, you will build trust. And trust is the building block of genuine relationships.

The biggest mental obstacle is the fact that this is not a quick fix. It requires patience. The fruits will take time to show. But they will be top-quality fruits!

This umbrella concept of building meaningful relationships dovetails into many of the other buttons on the remote.

Taking chances and risks: allowing people into your life can feel uncomfortable and vulnerable.

Self-talk: are you telling yourself they won't be interested in you? Or that it will be interesting to meet someone new?

Cultivating a curious and growth mindset: Let go of the idea that you need to be interesting for other people to like you. The best foundation for meaningful relationships is to be interested in them. Be curious, genuinely want to know about their world, their work, their story.

Time: Relationships need some investment of time. I know, you are time-poor. Set some realistic goals. Maybe 20 minutes, twice a week for some LinkedIn engagement, for texting or emailing some people you want to keep on your radar. Perhaps you can meet one person a week for coffee or lunch.

Giving back to the community: This is a fabulous way to connect with people you would not otherwise meet. At the same time, you gain a new experience, possibly develop your skills in a different way, and you help others.

Working with a mentor: This is an opportunity to build a very meaningful relationship with one significant person. On top of that, your mentor can help you build other relationships by coaching you on building relationships or by introducing you to other
people.

If you haven't already guessed, what I am talking about here is networking. That's right. Networking is not about using people or asking for favors. That brand of "networking" simply doesn't work. Genuine networking is about giving and sharing. It results in greater things than you could have dreamed up for yourself. The book you hold in your hands right now is an example of just that. When people collaborate, something magical happens. What could that mean for your career?

What can you add to this list?

Written By

Bernie McFarlane
Career Development Professional specialising in networking and job search. Connector of dots.

How do you remain in-charge of career growth?

Career Change Bingo

I know my transferable skills	I know my intent behind career change	I am exploring study options	I am creating many possible career selves and pathways	I am driven by curiosity
I interact with those who work in my target career/job	I am aware of the financial impact of career change	I know how much risk I can take	I volunteer or have a side-project	I'm actively considering side - project/ volunteering
I am willing to trust my instinct	My family is aware and supportive of the career change	I am building team of cheerleaders around me	I take inspiration from career change stories	I am aware of the business problems I solve
I know my strengths and weaknesses	I effectively leverage social media for research and networking	I explore how others have pivoted to a new career	I attend networking events aligning with career change objective	I have a mentor who can guide
I have completed a career assessment	I remain optimistic about the career change	I test career change ideas with my well wishers	I believe it is possible to change careers	I am committed to make career change a positive experience

Career Change Bingo

"Regardless of where you are in your career - whether you're just starting out, comfortably mid-career, or maybe approaching the twilight of your working years – the chances are you will have created patterns.

Maybe you stay in a job until you get bored then look for another, maybe you
stick around for 15 months before you start looking for something new, maybe you're waiting for a fairy godmother to pluck you out of the job you're in and take you somewhere new.... Well, this Career Change Bingo game might be just what you need to break out of your usual habits and ignite something new, bringing more consciousness to your career journey.

Instead of going it alone and repeating old patterns, the ideas in this game encourage you to speak to others and explore new possibilities mentors, encouragers, family members, networks. In fact, another interesting addition to this bingo might be to create a family tree of everybody's primary area of work who knows what you might find. A family tendency towards a certain industry? A particular skill that runs through your genes which you might be underutilising? Somebody who's previously held a role you might like to explore?

A hard truth of many careers is that we can feel like a passenger in a car that's being driven out of our control. We wait to be seen at work, wait for that tap on the shoulder about something new, hope that somehow the universe will provide us with an opportunity. By playing a game like Career Change Bingo, you'll feel like you're actually driving the car yourself. Crossing off the rows and columns will likely encourage you to explore new possibilities, talk to new people, and research alternative journeys."

Written By

Kathryn Jackson
Executive Coach | Facilitator | Author | Director of Careerbalance Ltd | Founder of The Great Recharge! Polite disruptor and life changer for everybody who wants to build confidence.

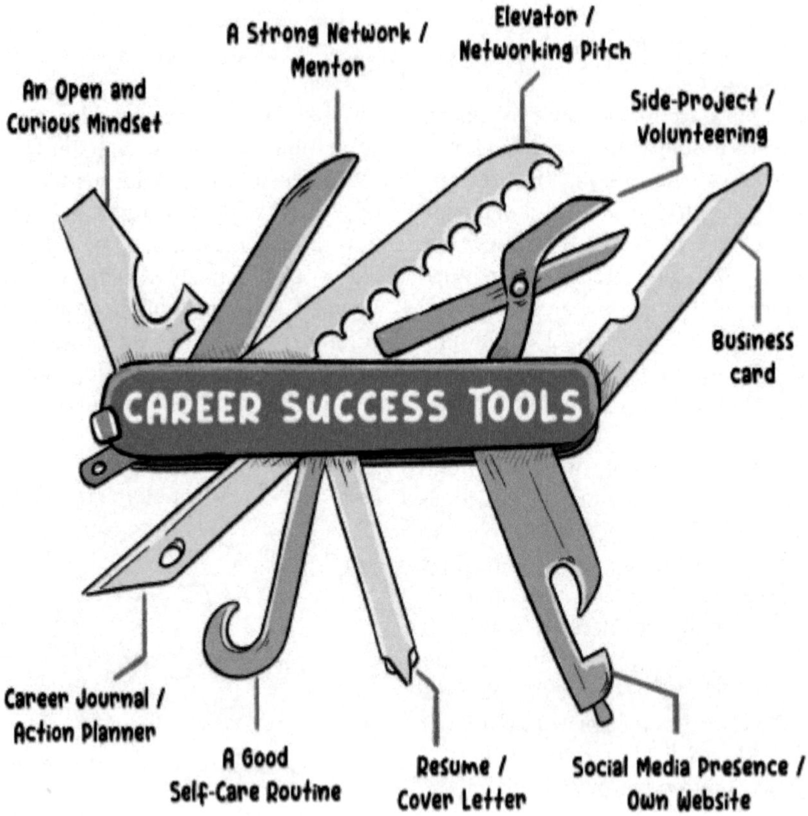
A Strong Network /
Mentor
Elevator /
Networking Pitch
An Open and
Curious Mindset
Side-Project /
Volunteering
Business
card
CAREER SUCCESS TOOLS
Career Journal /
Action Planner
A Good
Self-Care Routine
Resume /
Cover Letter
Social Media Presence /
Own Website

Career Success Tools

Growing up, MacGyver was a show that my family loved to watch. We loved how resourceful Richard Dean Anderson's character, MacGyver, was, and greatly admired his problem-solving mind. Without realizing it at the time, MacGyver's practical and hands-on style (and his casual, saving-the-world attitude) turned out to have more
influence on how I go about my career and life than I expected.

Most people take a linear approach when it comes to finding a job and building a career, as that's how we've been taught. Resume, cover letter, job sites, and maybe updating and networking on LinkedIn; perhaps not always in the same order, but still a linear approach. I, however, have always imagined I can play MacGyver when it comes to career building, being resourceful with a bit of fun. While I still write cover letters and prepare different versions of my resume, I also like to look for other creative ways to experiment. That's why this pocket knife illustration resonates with me. It is something that MacGyver would have in his pocket.

I remember I used to read the job advertisement section of the newspaper every week when jobs were still being advertised in printed newspapers. I would not only search for jobs in my industry but also read jobs for all other sectors. From a general manager role in the banking industry to a forklift driver position in a logistics industry, I would read them with great interest. Then I would imagine what skills I may need to apply for those jobs. I never applied for that forklift driver position. Not only does operating a forklift require a special license, but I'm also not a confident driver in general. The role was never going to be a good fit, but I had fun letting my imagination run wild with scenario planning. I became an imaginary MacGyver who was job hunting.

I soon realised that a strong resume and a good cover letter were not enough when applying for a job. A resume may get me in the door, but I would always need something else to close the deal. So, I began building my own "career pocketknife" to help me cut through the competition. Some of the tools that I acquired to customize my career pocketknife include voluntary experience, self-paced study, cultural understanding through traveling, and board/governance knowledge. Many of these tools are not directly related to my professional training, but they are immensely helpful.

I can clearly recall two important moments in my career when I had to use my career pocketknife during my interview to "close the deal." One of these key moments was so profound that I actually switched my career path as a result.

We can't deny that job hunting and career building can be hard, even soul-destroying at times after countless rejections. That's why acknowledging building a career is not a linear process is so important. The sooner we can do that, the sooner we can don our MacGyver hat and start building a career pocketknife of our own. And in the process, we will naturally develop our knowledge and skills, in both depth (our specialisation) and breadth (our understanding of life), for a successful career.

What can you add to this list?

Written By

Dr Suzi Chen
Self-Leadership Advocate, Impact Investor & Founder @ Notonos & Resilient Leadership Academy Developing resilient leaders with purposeful career through self-leadership.

Career Compass Box

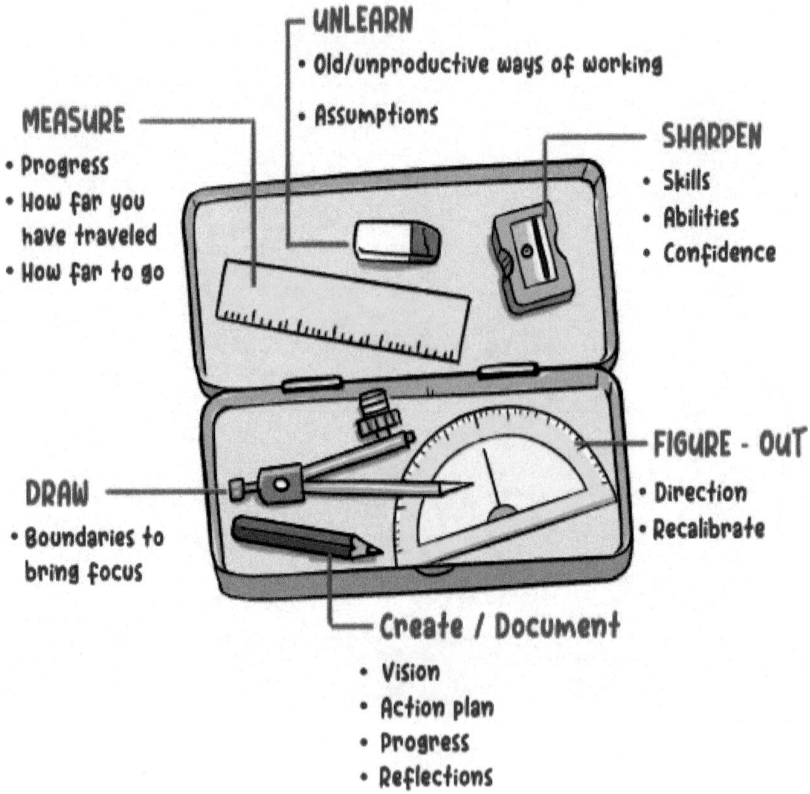
UNLEARN
• Old/unproductive ways of working
• Assumptions
MEASURE
• Progress
• How far you have traveled
• How far to go
SHARPEN
• Skills
• Abilities
• Confidence
FIGURE - OUT
• Direction
• Recalibrate
DRAW
• Boundaries to bring focus
Create / Document
• Vision
• Action plan
• Progress
• Reflections

Career Growth Compass Box

"Career Compass Box" provides a roadmap for individuals who want to achieve their professional goals. The Compass Box consists of five core elements, each designed to help people navigate the challenges and opportunities of today's work.

Let's define the tools in our "Career Compass Box":

- The first element of the compass box is "Sharpening," which emphasizes the importance of developing skills, abilities, and confidence.
- The second element of the compass box is "Measurement," and it's about tracking your progress and how far you've come in your career.
- The third element of the compass box is "Unlearn," or letting go of old skills and ways of working that no longer serve you.
- The fourth element of the compass box is "Drawing," and it's about setting boundaries and focusing on what's important.
- Finally, the fifth element of the compass is "Creation," and it's about envisioning your future, making plans, and taking action to make your vision a reality.

After executing a successful project in the USA for which I was awarded Employee of the Year award and flew to Australia (from the USA) to receive the award, I was promoted to Project Manager. I returned to India and started to work in this new role (for me and the offshore org).

The first tool that I used was "Measurement." I learned that I needed to improve my skills as a technical lead to work as a Project Manager (PM). A PM needs a different set of tools and techniques to handle the project, and my technical skills were an added advantage (and sometimes a disadvantage) to the project. Measuring myself and where I stood was the best thing I did.

The next tool I used from the compass was "Sharpening." Based on my measurement, I knew I needed additional skills to work efficiently as a Project Manager. I decided to sharpen my skills and get myself PMP (Project Management Professional) certified. The key was to get things in perspective on what needed to be done to get a PMP. Here, my other tools, like "Drawing" and "Unlearning," became beneficial. I sought help from a certified and experienced PMP, and he decided to mentor me.

We went to the drawing board and created a plan for myself, focusing on what I needed and helping me set goals to achieve my PMP. The first part of the goal was to unlearn some of the methods of how we handle projects. Unlearning was one of the most challenging things I had to take up. It would mean I need to go with what PMP says, not with my experience or instincts.

By now, I was doing well with the plan we had created, and it was time for "Creation" (my last tool in the compass box). The key was to focus on the plan and work towards the goal. My mentor was helpful during these times. From when I measured myself to when I finished my PMP, all my tools in the compass box helped me achieve my goal.

In conclusion, the "Career Compass Box" is a powerful tool for anyone looking to achieve their professional goals.

Do you have all the tools in your compass box? What is missing in the box?

Written By

Amit Khanna
TEDx Speaker. Mentor in Communication and Leadership. Helping professionals with the tools and strategies they need to communicate effectively and confidently.

Check each tool and reflect on how have you used it or how are you willing to use it?

Your Career = Skills + Strengths + Interests + Aptitudes

Unlimited Career Possibilities

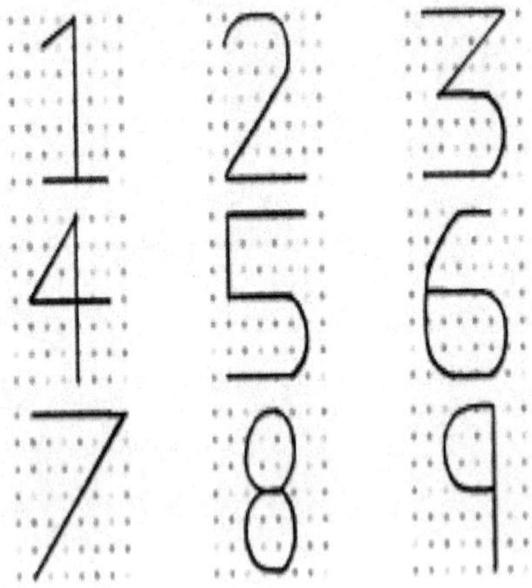

Unlimited Career Possibilities:

I love how this doodle shows how you can combine your skills, strengths, and interests to create possibilities for the future.

First, you need to identify and list your skills, strengths, and interests. If you'd like any support with this, a registered career professional can help you name and celebrate what makes you 'you'*.

Once you know them, link your skills, strengths, and interests together and see what ideas surface.

Old ideas? Resurrect and check them.

New ideas? Let them in.

Don't worry about realism at this stage. That can come later.

Decide which dots to connect and how to connect them. Shuffle the dots around. Mix and mash them together in different combinations and ways, in different scenarios, for different reasons and causes, according to what matters and what makes sense to you. Even if an idea doesn't seem to matter or make sense, don't automatically rule it out – if something lights you up, the meaning may arrive later.

If existing possibilities seem limited or don't appeal, don't worry. New options exist beyond what you can see or imagine right now. They will come into focus as you step forward into the future. Embrace a growth mindset (Dweck, 2006). Take positive action to grow your skills and interests – they are not fixed. When we grow, new possibilities materialise. So:

- Step out of your comfort zone.
- Take risks.
- Learn new things.
- Accept failure as part of the journey, a new segment of the crazy paving path (the one in Sir Dominic Cadbury's famous quote**) that stretches into your future.
- Stay curious and open to new possibilities.
- Get ready to share your skills and talents in new ways.

As you move forward, new options will emerge.

The fast-changing world presents new possibilities too. In the fourth industrial revolution, automation, globalisation, climate change, demographics, and changing attitudes and behaviours offer fresh ways for us to use our time, energy, and talents. The opportunity structure (Roberts, 1977) is shifting and evolving. New possibilities are appearing.

And, if you don't want to or can't decide between possibilities, you don't even have to choose. Not everyone devotes all their time and talent to one specific activity or cause. You could pursue a portfolio career, where you mix activities and ways of working (e.g., part-time, freelance, contract) to create a balance that's right for you. Or maybe you see yourself more as a multipotentialite (Rahayel, 2014), pursuing interests and passions in parallel, without it needing to make sense or lead to an end goal.

Exciting possibilities are out there. Are you ready to find and embrace them? Then step forward, discover, grow, learn, apply, and have fun along the way!

* A registered career professional can also help you explore other internal drivers, like your values, personality, and sense of purpose. Once you know these, even more options may emerge.

**"There's no such thing as a career path, it's crazy paving and you have to lay it yourself."

References

BBC Bitesize (2022) Portfolio careers – the new normal? Available at: https://www.bbc.co.uk/bitesize/articles/zktbn9q (Accessed: 21 August 2022).

Dweck, C. S. (2006) Mindset: The New Psychology of Success. New York: Random House Publishing Group.

National Careers Week (NCW) (2022) The Future of Work Guide. Available at: https://nationalcareersweek.com/2022fow/ (Accessed: 21 August 2022).

Rahayel, A. (2014) On being a multipotentialite. Available at: https://www.youtube.com/watch?v=N6G3QcpoJd4 (Accessed: 21 August 2022).

Roberts, K. (1977) 'The social conditions, consequences and limitations of career guidance', British Journal of Guidance and Counselling, 5(1), pp. 1-9.

Scott, K. (2018) Did You Know (Shift Happens) - 2018 Remix. Available at: https://www.youtube.com/watch?v=TwtS6Jy3ll8 (Accessed: 21 August 2022).

Written By

Lis McGuire
Registered Career Development Professional (RCDP), Founder of Sunrise Career Guidance, & Creator of Shape of Career cards.

Do you want to create unlimited career possibilities?

1. Take a large butcher paper.
2. Make a list of skills, strengths, and interests you have.
3. Arrange them similar to the doodle.
4. Connected 9 skills, strengths, and interests.
5. Zoom out and brainstorm a career that aligns with the connected skills, strengths, and skills.
6. Repeat with new set of 9 skills, strengths, and skills.

WE SPEND

90,000

hours at work.

Make it Worth.

90,000 hours

Oooph. 90,000 is a big number. Assuming a 40-hour work week and 4 weeks of annual leave each year, that is 46 years of working.

Did you know that "85% of people in full-time jobs globally are unhappy in their jobs" - Gallup? Oh, and:

- 67% of adult Australians are overweight or obese.
- 45% of Australian adults will be affected by mental illness at some time in their life.
- 44% of marriages globally end in divorce.
- The working poor are over 10% in some countries in Europe.
- 51% of Australians experience loneliness every week.

That says to me that the way we work is broken.

How did you come to do the work you're doing anyway? Let me guess, an important person in your formative years said you would be good at and should be a 'insert here'. Or maybe you fell into your role? Did your work find you?

If any of the above resonates with you, it's likely that your job is filled with tasks you're good at, and your day is filled with what others want you to do.

I encourage you to take a different approach that includes five steps.
First, give thought to why you work. Most will say they have to or they need the money, and I encourage you to dig deeper. How you answer this question shapes the experiences you can have while working.

Everyone aspires to something; that might be to be happy, successful, or a good human. Whatever it may be, we learn over time what it takes to be what we aspire to. These beliefs become rules, and we have to follow our own rules. Evaluating our own rules allows us to see different opportunities and take different actions.

Life design is next. Know what you want to experience, who you want to share it with, and the finances required to pay for it all. Then work out what level of health and well-being you will need to physically be able to do it. It is also important to think about who you want to be as you live this life. Could that be as a generous, kind, loving human? That's up to you. When you have designed your life, work can be a vehicle that connects you to the people and activities that are important to you while you generate the financial resources to pay for it.

Job design is next. A job might be seen as a group of tasks. Most people's days are filled with tasks that they are good at. Unfortunately, that is not often the same as what they love doing or is important to them. Connect again with those tasks. Every day with just a few more tasks you love doing or are important to you is a great day.

Finally, write it all down as your ideal job. Writing it down gives you a tangible tool to create Work with Meaning so you can be your best and do your best work. Go for twenty features and/or characteristics. This requires you to go beyond what you want to do and include how you want to do it and with whom you want to do it with.

Individuals who Work with Meaning have a ripple effect across their communities because they are better partners, parents, siblings, friends, colleagues, etc. Make your 90,000 hours count!

1. Australian Institute of Health & Wellfare. https://www.aihw.gov.au/reports/australias-health/overweight-and-obesity
2. Better Health Channel https://www.betterhealth.vic.gov.au/health/ServicesAndSupport/mental-illness-statistics
3. Unified Lawyers https://www.unifiedlawyers.com.au/blog/global-divorce-rates-statistics/
4. Tutor2U https://www.tutor2u.net/economics/reference/working-poverty
5. Australian Loneliness Report 2018https://www.psychweek.org.au/wp/wp-content/uploads/2018/11/Psychology-Week-2018-Australian-Loneliness-Report.pdf

Written By

Brian Klindworth
Melbourne boy born to an American Dad and English Mum who co-parents and loves sport. He also works as a Career Coach and helps people to Be their best and Do their best work.

Out of 90,000 hours, how much have you already used?

How do you plan to spend the remaining hours?

Tribe and Why It's Important

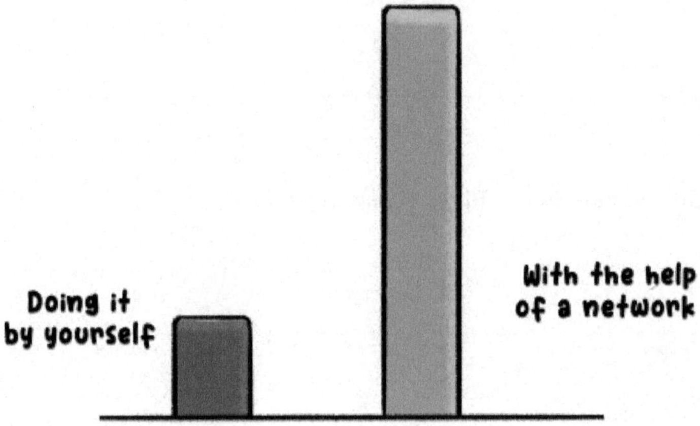

Tribe and Why It's Important

If you're like me, when you first looked for a job, the idea of networking was foreign.

It still sounds like a strange, formal, and slightly sniffy term for something that can be as simple as catching up with an old boss for a coffee, emailing someone you got talking to at a conference, or volunteering to do something you enjoy professionally – for free.

These are all things I've done when I've been looking for a way to break out of a career fog or find a new direction – and these actions have all led me to find exciting opportunities.

The "old boss coffee catch-up" led to an offer to mentor one of her team in recruitment.

I Googled the email address of an online job board editor I met at a conference and told her the bits of my background that were relevant for her to know. All I then said was that I enjoyed reading what she wrote and would love to be kept in mind if something suitable came up. The editor contacted me immediately as she needed help answering emails from job seekers.

Volunteering to contribute articles to magazines led me to more paid work, including eventually writing career pieces for The Australian.

So, what happens when you look for a job alone vs. getting out amongst it with other people?

Sitting behind a screen solo, churning out application after application means you're only accessing jobs that are already created – and by that point, you will be competing against hundreds.

If you're out talking to people, it's more likely that you're joining a discussion about a problem they're having – and by being on the spot, presenting yourself as a solution.

Among other things, you're demonstrating that you're trustworthy, proactive, that you have good communication skills, and can solve a problem. When you make these claims on a resume, they can appear like keywords you've been told to weave into a resume – and indistinguishable from the claims every other job seeker makes on paper.

Networking can be as easy as being interested in other people and a good listener. You don't need to beat your chest with your elevator pitch, as what you do or want to do or can do often comes up naturally as a question during the conversation.

If you've made the right impression and a genuine connection, the person you meet can become your eyes and ears in their company when the HR email comes around saying, "we're hiring – does anybody know anybody who can....?"
Often, you'll find you'll be considered for a role this way, even if you don't have the perfect experience on paper. Cultural fit and the right attitude are always important. The assumption is that you'll be a good fit for the team if someone good has recommended you.

The hidden peril of job seeking alone is that your world closes in.

You can find yourself giving up as you become a product of your last rejection when you try to figure out what you're doing wrong by yourself, instead of surrounding yourself with people with the growth mindset you need to have.

Your network can be thinking about how you can help them in ways that you never know at that point in time.

What does tribe mean to you?

Written By

Karalyn Brown
Career Coach + Founder: InterviewIQ & Straight to Shortlist Challenge: Learn how to take control of your job search and get 5 meetings with 5 employers in 5 weeks!

Who is included in your tribe?

What do you do to strengthen your tribe?

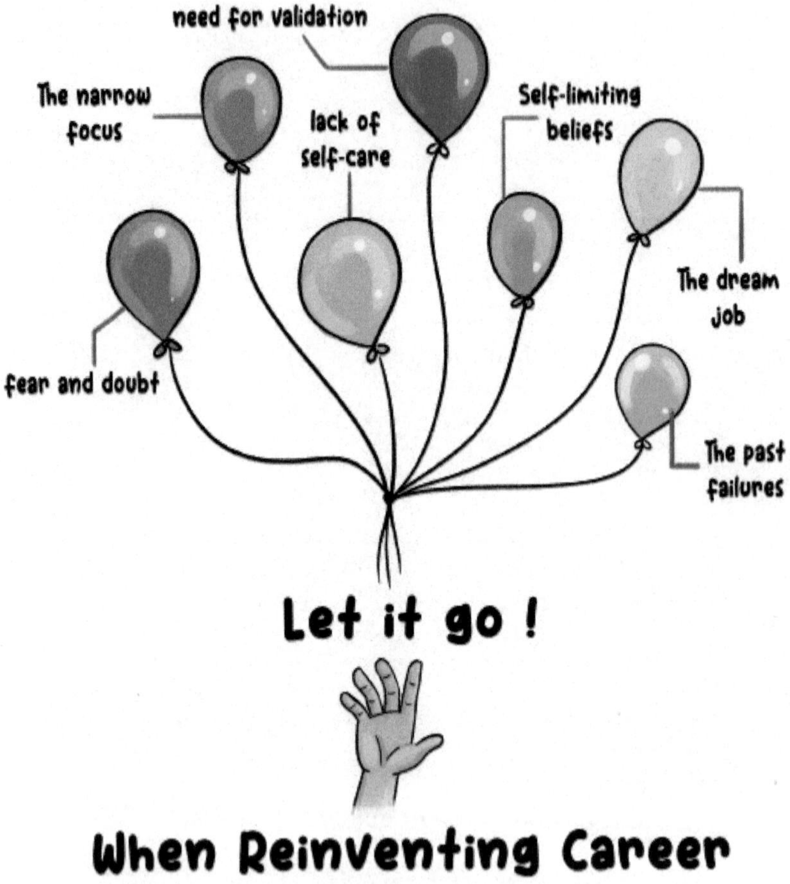
need for validation
The narrow focus
lack of self-care
Self-limiting beliefs
The dream job
fear and doubt
The past failures
Let it go !
When Reinventing Career

Releasing the Balloons of Career Reinvention: Letting Go of the Things

Picture this: you're holding onto seven brightly coloured balloons, each one representing a piece of baggage that's been weighing you down in your career. Fear and doubt, the need for validation, a narrow focus, the idea of a "dream job", self-limiting beliefs, past failures, and a lack of self-care. It's time to let go of these balloons and watch them float away, making room for a new, lighter you.

Let's start with fear and doubt. This balloon is a murky, grey colour, but once you release it, you'll see how much brighter the world can be. Don't let your fears and doubts hold you back from pursuing the career of your dreams. Take a deep breath, gather your courage, and let that balloon fly away.

Next up is the need for validation. This balloon is a bright pink, and it might be the hardest one to let go of. It's natural to want validation and approval from others, but you can't let that control your career decisions. Trust in yourself and your abilities, and let that balloon float away.

The narrow focus balloon is a muted brown color. When you're too focused on one specific path, you might miss out on other opportunities that could be even more fulfilling. Don't let that happen to you. Release the narrow focus balloon and open yourself up to new possibilities.

The dream job balloon is a bright, sparkling gold. While it's important to have aspirations and goals, don't let the idea of a "dream job" hold you back. Sometimes, the best opportunities come from unexpected places. Let go of that balloon and be open to new possibilities.

Self-limiting beliefs are represented by a balloon that's a murky, greenish-gray color. We all have beliefs about ourselves and our abilities, but sometimes those beliefs hold us back. Let go of those self-limiting beliefs and start believing in yourself and your potential.

The past failures balloon is a dark, stormy blue. It's easy to get caught up in the past and let our failures define us, but it's important to learn from those experiences and move on. Release that balloon and let go of any negative baggage from your past.

Finally, the lack of a self-care balloon is a soft, calming pink. Taking care of yourself is essential for success in any career. Don't neglect your physical or mental health. Release that balloon and prioritize self-care in your life.

As you release each of these balloons, take a moment to reflect on how much lighter you feel. You're no longer weighed down by fear, self-doubt, or past failures. You're free to pursue your dreams and explore new opportunities. So, go ahead and let go of those balloons. You'll be amazed at how high you can soar when you're not weighed down by all that baggage.

Credits: Originated with CHATGPT AI, polished by Naishadh Gadani

CHATGTP is property of OpenAI

What are you holding onto?

Written By

Naishadh Gadani
Engineer turned Career Practitioner. Author. Doodler. Presenter. Non-TEDx Speaker. Helping people design their careers.

What will allow you to let go off the things that are holding you back?

Plug the Leaks. Fulfill On Your Potential.

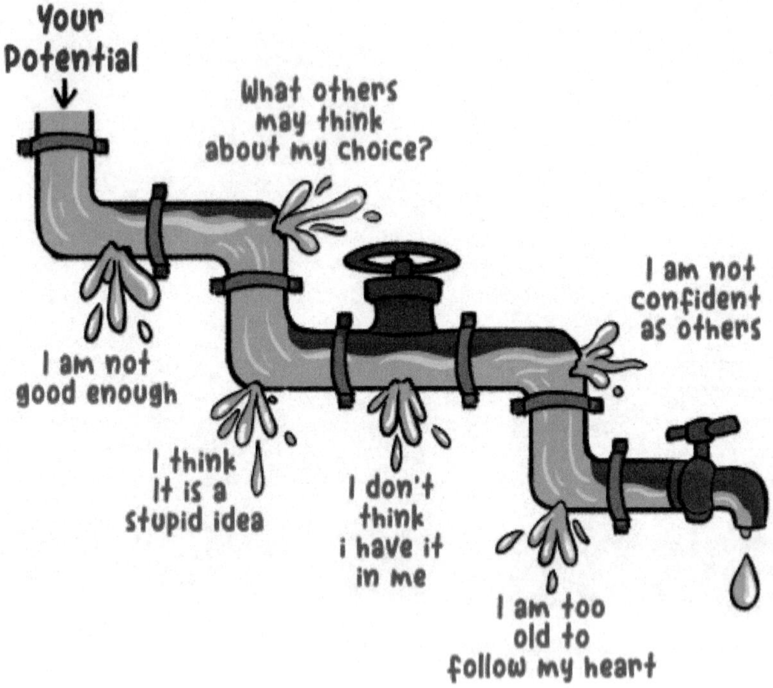

Plug the leaks. Fulfil On Your potential

I was a high achiever in my school days, always ahead of the game in everything I got involved with - be it studies, dance, sports, public speaking, and much more. After becoming an Electronics Engineer in 2005, I moved to a new country to follow the love of my life. No one knew my old identity here. I got busy working on my goals like pursuing a postgraduate degree, permanent visa, buying the first home, starting a family, building a great career, and the list goes on. In doing all these, I was mostly trying to fit in and was staying away from standing out like I used to in my early years.

Just like Naishadh's career doodle here, I didn't realise I was drifting further away from achieving my true potential as I was worried about others' opinions or not wanting to rock the boat. Being a migrant, I was just trying to blend in all the time. Fast forward 15 years, I had a lot of time at hand during the first year of the COVID pandemic and grieving for losing my father unexpectedly, I came to realise that I had been living in my head a lot for the past many years.

To plug the leaks in my pipeline of achieving my true potential, I took numerous coaching and mentoring programs, read self-help books, listened to leading podcasts, and networked with successful people in the area to find out how they did it all. One common theme emerged for me is that one who follows their passion, doesn't care about others' opinions, just keeps taking action, and repeats until they achieve their goals - reaches their true potential. It has been 3 years since than I can see that I am finally back on track to achieve my true potential. I am less worried about what people will say and more focused on what action I can take next. This has been a game-changer for me. I dare you to try it as well.

From my own lived experiences, I am a true believer that our potential is as much as we believe it to be. Achieving true potential is all about taking action in the right direction! If we slow ourselves down with worries about what others may think about our choices, doubting our own abilities, or judging our own potential by age - all these factors will directly impact us if we can realise our potential to the fullest.

The most important aspect for achieving our dreams or goals is to act. Another important aspect to be aware of is that opinions and the inner voice will never go away completely. We just have to learn to live with them and keep taking action towards our goals anyway, no matter how big or small! Overcoming the feeling of imposter was the first thing I tackled successfully in my journey to achieving my full potential. By attending numerous panel discussions, coaching programs, reading books, and listening to podcasts on Imposter Syndrome, I concluded that I will need not to fear my inner voice, it's there for a reason. I learned to have control over it, rather than let my inner voice control my actions. A lot of successful people experience imposter feelings from time to time. The aim is to not get rid of it as it protects our psychological safety in a way. I gave my inner voice a name - 'Jenny'. Jenny sometimes goes crazy, and I calm her down. I listen to her, which makes her feel better, and then she becomes quiet and lets me take the action I need to take.

As I progress in life, my goals evolve, and I am evolving with them. The next leak I need to fix is 'people-pleasing'. I am working on creating and practicing healthy boundaries.

I am aware that even when I have mastered these skills, many situations will continue to arise where my boundaries will be tested. Therefore, it is a continuous process of plugging these leaks and keeping those plugs in place. The more leaks we plug, the closer we come to realising our potential!

Reflect on the doodle. What are some of the leaks do you identify that doesn't fulfil your potential?

Written By

Jalpa Bhavsar
Speaker | Mentor | Cybersecurity Leader Helping organisations secure their infrastructure, data and people.

What will allow you to let go off the things that are holding you back?

Career Growth Spinning Wheel

Career Growth Spinning Wheel

"Turn! Turn! Turn (To Everything There Is a Season)" is a song **Written By** Pete Seeger which became an international hit in the 1960s for the American folk rock band, the Byrds.

The song draws on the biblical Book of Ecclesiastes:

"To everything there is a season, and a time to every purpose under the heaven:

A time to be born, and a time to die; a time to plant, a time to reap that which is planted.

A time to kill, and a time to heal; a time to break down, and a time to build up."

This song is a reminder that the wheel of life is designed to keep on turning.

When the career area of your life is going through a difficult season, rest assured it provides you with the potential to turn it into an opportunity.

Ray's Career Wheel Turning Point

While driving home from the office late one Friday, 42-year-old Ray received a phone call from his manager, Angela. ***"Don't come back Monday, the company has just abolished your job,"*** she told Ray.

This was a massive unexpected blow for the dedicated and loyal Ray.

"A time to be born, a time to die, a time to break down and a time to build up"

These lyrics reflected where Ray now found himself on the Career Wheel.

Ray now had a choice. He could go home and bring his misery through the front door, drown his sorrows with his favourite red wine, and then curl up in a fetal position.

As an avid reader and attendee of seminars from the motivational world, Ray knew it was his defining moment to stand up and be counted.

You see, Ray knew deep down that he had been stagnating for years, rotting away in cubicle land when he harbored a burning desire to do something else with his life.

Ray had a dream to be a motivational speaker, an author, and to run his own business.

However, the financial stability from a regular paycheck that paid his mortgage, education, and fed his family was a chain he could not break.

Ray's career wheel had been stuck on the "time to go" position for years, but he couldn't take that step.

When we can't take that much-wanted step, life somehow intervenes and turns the wheel for us, even though it looks like it's being done to us.

So, his wheel had landed on the "don't come back" position, and he now found himself out the door.

Life's wheel had decided it was time for Ray's employee career to die and his entrepreneurial journey to be born.

Today, Ray enjoys a deeply rewarding and satisfying life as an author, helping others become authors, and build a business from their books.

To follow the rhythm of life as it ebbs and flows, be patient and remember that there is a time for everything.

What does each section mean to you? Act, Pause, Reflect, Assess, Recharge.

Written By

Tony Pisanelli
Tony Pisanelli is a Career Transformation Strategist and International Best-Selling Author who consults with C-Suite and senior executives.

What does each section mean to you? Act, Pause, Reflect, Assess, Recharge.

In Career

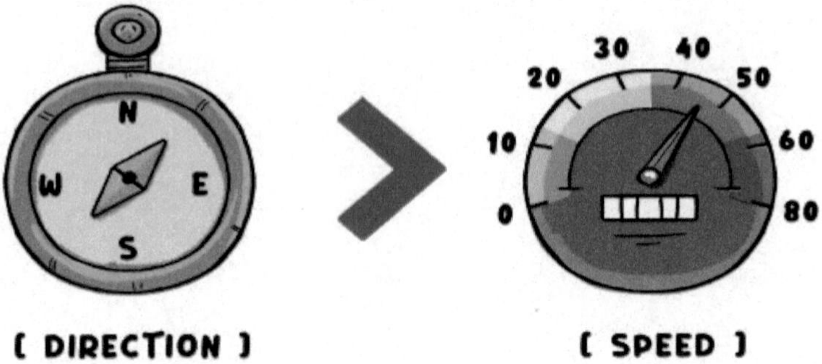

Direction > Speed

When it comes to career development, the most common advice is often to work hard, be ambitious, and move up the career ladder as quickly as possible. However, it's essential to understand that career direction is more important than speed. In other words, it's more important to know where you're going than to rush towards your goals without a clear plan.

Direction means having a clear vision of your career goals, understanding your strengths, weaknesses, interests, and values, and aligning them with the right opportunities. When you have a clear direction, you can make informed decisions, set realistic goals, and stay focused on what matters most.

On the other hand, speed refers to the pace at which you're moving in your career. While it's natural to want to progress quickly and achieve your goals as soon as possible, this can sometimes lead to making hasty decisions, taking on roles that aren't the right fit, or sacrificing your long-term goals for short-term gains.

Here are a few reasons why direction is more important than speed in your career:

1. **Direction helps you find your purpose:** When you have a clear sense of direction, you're better able to identify your purpose and the impact you want to make in your career. This clarity can help you stay motivated, focused, and committed to your goals, even when the going gets tough.
2. **Direction leads to better decision-making:** When you know where you're going, it's easier to make informed decisions about the opportunities that come your way. You can assess whether a particular job, project, or promotion aligns with your long-term goals and whether it's worth the time and effort.
3. **Direction helps you avoid burnout:** When you're solely focused on speed, it's easy to burn out and lose sight of what matters most. By contrast, when you have a clear direction, you can pace yourself, prioritize your workload, and avoid overcommitting yourself.
4. **Direction fosters lifelong learning:** When you have a clear sense of direction, you're more likely to seek out opportunities for growth and development that align with your goals. You're also more likely to stay curious, ask questions, and learn from others, all of which can help you become a better professional over time.

In conclusion, while speed may be important in some contexts, career direction is more important in the long run. By taking the time to define your career goals and align them with your interests, values, and strengths, you can set yourself up for success and fulfillment over the course of your career.

Credits: Originated with CHATGPT AI, polished by Naishadh Gadani

CHATGTP is property of OpenAI

Reflect on your career journey so far. What have you valued - direction or speed?

Written By

Naishadh Gadani
Engineer turned Career Practitioner. Author. Doodler. Presenter. Non-TEDx Speaker. Helping people design their careers.

How has it served you?

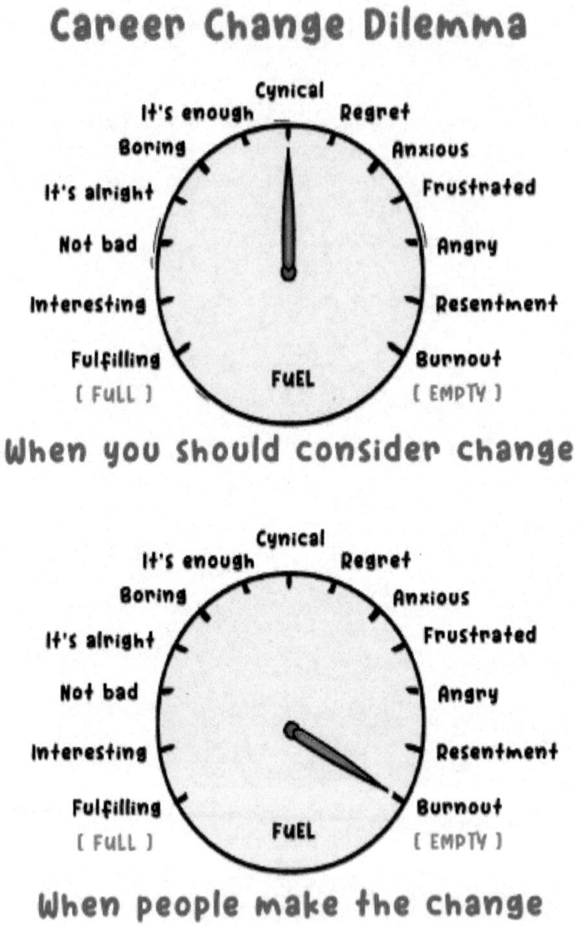
Career Change Dilemma
Cynical
It's enough
Regret
Boring
Anxious
It's alright
Frustrated
Not bad
Angry
Interesting
Resentment
Fulfilling
[FULL]
FUEL
Burnout
[EMPTY]
When you should consider change
Cynical
It's enough
Regret
Boring
Anxious
It's alright
Frustrated
Not bad
Angry
Interesting
Resentment
Fulfilling
[FULL]
FUEL
Burnout
[EMPTY]
When people make the change

Career Change Dilemma

Change should be considered when you get to 'boring' on the fuel gauge.

You might be able to negotiate more challenging projects, a leadership role, or a secondment into a completely different area.
Cynical is a hard mindset to get out of. It infiltrates every part of your day.

You might notice yourself becoming withdrawn and disengaged, or the opposite - quick to challenge and reluctant to go with the flow of new initiatives.

It impacts our relationships, and not just at work. It impacts all parts of our life - this is not just a job dilemma, it's a life dilemma.
From cynical onwards, our parasympathetic nervous system starts to go into overdrive. We feel stressed before we even get out of bed to get ready for work! We are in a constant state of questioning ourselves and our employer, which adds a huge mental load to our day. We might be scanning job sites on our lunch break. If so, we have already broken up with our job, we have emotionally exited. One foot in, one foot out. In this state, we feel duplicitous; it takes so much extra energy to appear engaged when your heart is just not in it.

It's okay to want to leave your job. But consider the legacy you want to leave and plan your exit accordingly. Waiting until 'burnout' on the dial risks damage to our relationships, our reputation, and our ability to effectively transition out of our role.

Big career decisions, like leaving your job, require full focus and space. We don't want to make this decision under pressure when we aren't feeling 100% well or clear. We want it to be an empowered choice to exit, not a desperate escape.

Burnout happened to me post-Covid. And this led me to leave my job and start my own business! It wasn't Covid that did it - I had inklings of cynicism a few months before, but I was stuck in the survival cycle* of my workplace. My body was sending me signals via my hormones that something wasn't right. I had reached out to a Coach, knowing that I needed some kind of objective sounding board to bounce the inklings with (because I couldn't have this kind of open conversation with my manager). But having Covid, and returning to work far too soon, taught me a lot about my physical and emotional limits. I had 'recovered', I was back at work, but I was struggling to keep it all up in the air. I was constantly angry at home, I was ultra-sensitive to light and noise, I was foggy at work and making silly mistakes in my emails. I really thought I was starting to go crazy, and I knew I needed a longer break. I saw my GP, who gave me very little to work with ("rest"). So, I accessed a Counsellor via my Employee Assistance Program. I explained to her what was going on.

Am I depressed?! Is there something more sinister underlying this?

She explained that I was still in recovery. My body was so focused on healing, that any additional stimulus (online meetings, screaming toddlers, the blaring credits to a kids cartoon) was completely overloading me. I was overstimulated. I needed time to heal. I needed to calm my nervous system. What she told me was some of the best insight I had gained over the course of my career thus far (oh, to have known this as a beginning teacher!). It made so much sense. I was instantly angry at my employer for expecting me to return to work so soon. I was furious at the culture of overwork and 'busy-ness' that we are sucked into. I started on a journey to reclaim my health, my creativity, and my work/life balance.

This included adopting a morning yoga practice, followed by journaling and a regular acupuncture session. It was my acupuncturist who revealed to me my stuck chi – literally a lack of flow. She encouraged me to return to my creative pursuits as well as nourishing my body. And she agreed with what the counsellor had told me. It was all starting to make sense.

Armed with a new appreciation for my body's intelligence (and how often do we actively ignore those warning signs?!) I set out on an 8-month process to transition from employee to solopreneur.
I was still cynical over the ensuing months. I still had moments of anger and resentment. I was the one piping up more often in meetings. To be honest, I felt a new sense of freedom. I was stepping into an authenticity I hadn't been permitted previously.

If someone had shown me this doodle at the beginning of 2022, I might have avoided burnout. Covid may not have hit me quite so hard. I might have garnered more courage to have those difficult but ultimately freeing conversations with my manager. But I'm a big believer in things working out the way they're meant to. I'm revelling in the creativity and freedom of being self-employed. I am ultimately grateful to have experienced the dial!

*We will remain in survival mode for as long as we choose to remain in survival mode.

Reflecting on the doodle, at which stage did you change your career?

Written By

Alana Lane, RPCDP - The Lane Method
Career Counsellor and Consultant
Listening. Learning. Storysharing

The Power of Curiosity

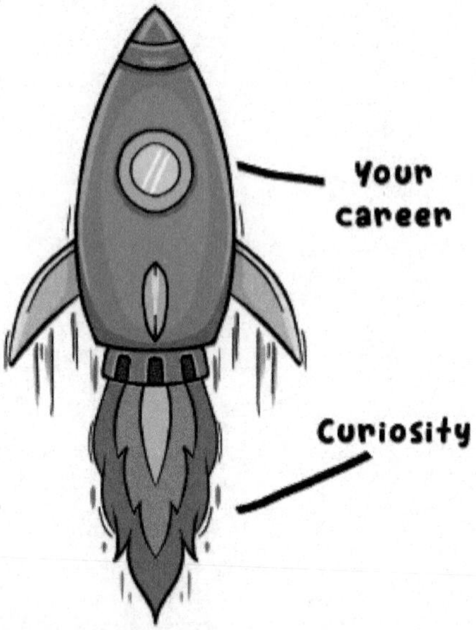

"Curiosity is the fire that propels career to greater heights"
- Naishadh Gadani

The Power Of Curiosity

Curiosity may have "killed the cat," but it certainly doesn't kill your career - quite the opposite. It's a crucial career skill that has the power to propel your career onwards and upwards, as Naishadh sums up in this wonderful image.

Modern-day careers are no longer linear and predictable. They are complex journeys full of unexpected twists and turns. An individual's mindset, which includes their curiosity, is one of the most important factors in determining their ability to adapt to these unpredictable times. In the theory of career adaptability, Savickas (2005) proposes four dimensions: career concern, career control, career curiosity, and career confidence. An individual's curiosity is the fuel to fire their motivation, both to explore the world around them but also to understand themselves better.

By embracing curiosity, individuals are more empowered to navigate their career journey. It has certainly played a significant part in my own. In fact, I recently wrote a post on LinkedIn about the power of curiosity in my own career:

"Whilst running on holiday last week, it got me thinking about career planning and how limiting it can be to become fixated with the final destination (the job title) rather than fully embracing the journey along the way.
Whenever I run, I have a vague destination in mind (last week it was a castle!) but I'm always led by my curiosity to see what I can discover along the way. Sometimes, like last week, my inquisitiveness leads to spectacular views and beautiful moments of silence amongst nature. But it also led to soaking wet feet and the odd dead end, but I still made it to the castle!

The twists and turns of my career, just like when I run, have led to some of the highlights, rich learning opportunities, amazing collaborations, and unexpected achievements. Even the tricky bits and dead ends have been opportunities for personal growth and a chance to develop my resilience and self-reflection."

As a Careers Coach myself, I always encourage young people to explore and be curious. It is one of the most important things for them to nurture in their journey through life. Curiosity keeps us moving forwards, leads us down new paths, opens new doors, and reveals exciting adventures. It's amazing what you can discover about yourself, who you can meet, and what you can create if you have the courage to be curious.

Curiosity is at the very heart of positive career development in modern-day careers.

What are you curious about?

How have you used curiosity in career development?

Written By

Katherine Jennick
Registered Career Development Professional (RCDP) and Creator of the award winning What's Your Strength?® cards - empowering people to recognise, celebrate and share strengths.

What do you do to remain curious?

Career

Career Expectations and Reality

How many people leave school expecting to have a very clear career trajectory, just like an escalator, with a smooth upward journey? Yet the reality of the career journey for many people can be better described as riding a roller coaster.

I'll put my hand up to this. I left school, went to university, and got my teaching qualification. The beginning of my teaching career was exciting, and I had my whole life mapped out in a smooth upward trajectory, just like as you head towards the top of the roller coaster. Or so I thought.

What I didn't consider at the time was how life throws curve balls, or how once the "honeymoon period" of a new role or career is over, you can suddenly find yourself hurtling down that rollercoaster, hanging on afraid that with any bump you might fall off at any moment. Perhaps feeling that you have lost control over your emotions, and not being able to see around the bends to predict what was coming next.

There are times when people accept a job offer expecting the role is going to be a certain way, yet only to discover once they are onboarded, the reality of the role turns out to be very different.

Transitions, whether planned or forced, can leave a person feeling this way about their career. Perhaps the transition encompasses a change in location, social groups, support networks or even a loss of sense of identity because a person's sense of self was heavily entwined with their work role.

As a former military spouse, I found myself experiencing the highs, lows, twists, and turns of my own career roller coaster on more than one occasion. Like many military spouses around the world, I faced the challenges of adapting to life in a military environment, away from family and the country where I grew up. Supporting my former husband's postings, including living in Germany for three years, and his later struggles during his transition to civilian life, meant that I gave up my chosen teaching career, leaving me with a sense of loss of identity. I struggled for some time to discover how to describe skills and knowledge from teaching as transferrable to other career pathways.

What can we do to manage and sustain ourselves during those times when we are travelling along the low points of the rollercoaster?

Below are strategies that may assist:

During the job search process:

- Research the job role, company, and its culture before applying for a position – networking and informational interviewing are great ways of finding out more about a role and company/ industry During the interview, ask questions such as:

- What does an average day in this role look like?

- How will you support the team if COVID-19 forces employees to work from home?

Sustaining hopefulness when times are tough:

- List 3 things that attracted you to your current role

- How do you currently enjoy yourself at work?

- Which of your qualities do you most enjoy using?

- Think about a time you faced a challenge and overcame it. What strengths and strategies did you use to be successful? How can you use those strengths and strategies in different challenging situations?

Written By

Jennifer (Jenn) Barfield RPCDP, PCDAA, CHATP:
Career Development Professional. Empowering people to sustain action-oriented hope. Specialises in Veteran and Military Spouse career journeys.

What were your expectations at the start of your career?

How did it turnout?

What have you learnt from your career journey so far?

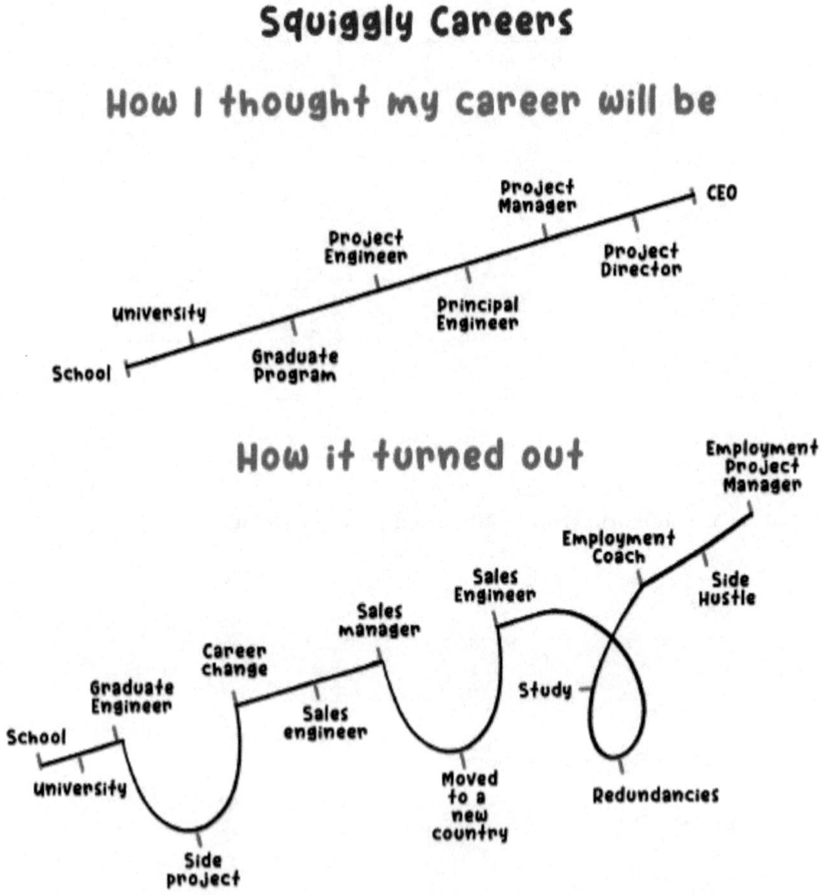
Squiggly Careers
How I thought my career will be
School
University
Graduate Program
Project Engineer
Principal Engineer
Project Manager
Project Director
CEO
How it turned out
School
University
Graduate Engineer
Side project
Career change
Sales engineer
Sales manager
Moved to a new country
Sales Engineer
Study
Redundancies
Employment Coach
Side Hustle
Employment Project Manager

Squiggly Careers

"Have you ever noticed that life never goes exactly the way you expected it to? When we're at school, one of the many messages about careers is that we're likely to start at the bottom somewhere, journey our way up, and then, if we work hard, we'll likely finish at the top. I'm sure you've already noticed that life just isn't that simple. In fact, the idea of traditional straight-line progression can often rely on us being driven by the idea of being paid more every time we're promoted up the ladder, but in reality, this is often not quite the case.

This concept can work for some people, but for others, there will be different things that are important to us during our career lifetime:

- You might fall in love with somebody who lives in another country – suddenly you'll take any job you can to be with them...
- You decide to raise a family and realise that juggling your family with work commitments means a change of role until the children grow up...
- Your elderly parents need support, so you move to a new city to look after them and take what you can get...
- A friend starts a new business, and you decide to join them on their adventure...
- You decide to take a new role so you can develop skills which aren't possible to use in your current one...
- The economy demands that for a while you need to work two jobs to make ends meet...
- You decide to study something new to boost your CV...

As you can see, there are so many reasons that a straightforward "up the ladder" might not be right for you, and these are just a few ideas. At the end of the day, the most important thing about career choices is that they give you (mostly) good days at work. If the balance of positive to negative days is right, then it's likely to be a good career move for you. It's unlikely that all of your wants and desires will be filled by one job for the whole of your life because we change so much as we grow up, so a squiggly career like this can be part of the answer.

On top of this, the world is always changing, and the dream job that you'd like to try might not even exist yet – but when it does, you'll no doubt want to step away from your linear progression to try it out! Whether your career moves up the traditional ladder or taking a crazy paving sort of approach, make sure that they fulfill you and play to your strengths. Ask yourself questions like: what matters the most to me right now? What are the skills that I'd like to use more (or less) in my work? What's changed in my life that might require me to change up my job too? Where have I seen a role that I might covet?

Bringing this sort of consciousness to career changes means that you're less likely to have a wild and unruly CV with random changes and plot twists, both of which might put your future career in jeopardy by signaling to employers that you're flighty or unsure of what you want to do."

Has your career progressed in a linear or squiggly fashion?

Written By

Kathryn Jackson
Executive Coach | Facilitator | Author | Director of Careerbalance Ltd | Founder of The Great Recharge! Polite disruptor and life changer for everybody who wants to build confidence.

What are some of the highs and lows of your career?

What did you learn from the highs and lows?

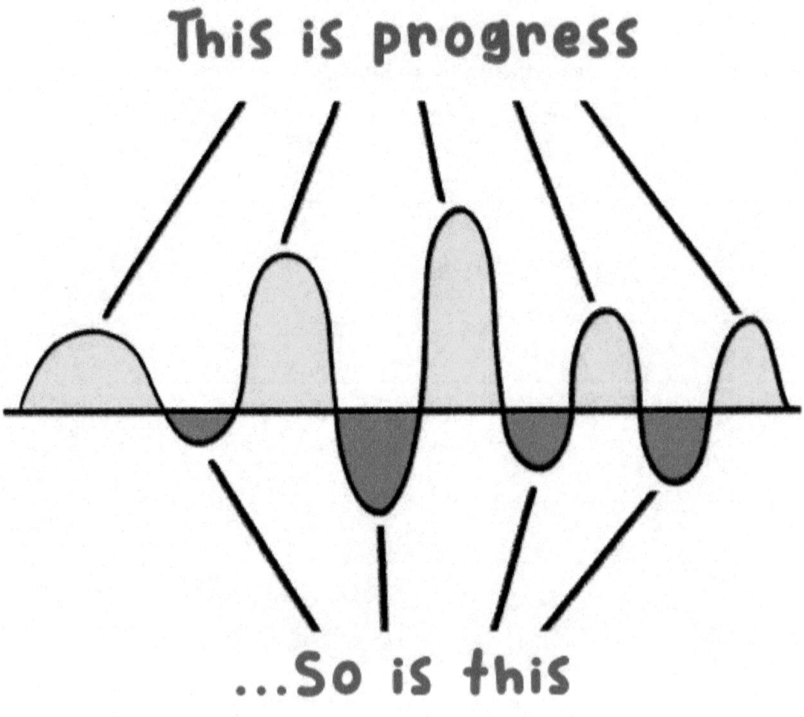
This is progress
...So is this

This Is Also Progress

The job search process is long and difficult. Finding a job that matches your skills, values, and career goals takes time and effort.

Understanding what you want out of your career and what you need to do to achieve it will make progress in your career and work search simpler. Progress is developing an understanding of the work and organisations you want to engage with. What are you looking for in your next employer? Do you want a company with work-life balance?
A company with lots of growth opportunities? A company that values creativity? All of these things should be considered before starting your search. Once you have identified what you are looking for, it becomes much easier to narrow the search to jobs and organisations that might be a good fit for you. Understanding what you want to do and whom you want to work for will support the creation of plans and help to become opportunity aware and responsive.

Progress is developing a clear understanding of your abilities and worth to potential employers. By understanding what skills and capabilities you have, it will help to underpin applications and make job interview preparation more straightforward and effective. Making progress is acknowledging what you need to work on. You should be honest with yourself about the skills and abilities that you have, as well as those that you need to develop.

Progress is orchestrating and engaging with your natural support system and network to promote yourself as an ideal employee looking for work. This is a simple exercise when you understand precisely what you want and what you have to offer.

Informational interviews are a great way to learn about career pathways and develop knowledge of the labor market you wish to enter. Actively engaging with organisations after the interview to get feedback on your performance and express your gratitude for the opportunity is also a worthwhile exercise. It helps to stay on the radar of the person making the hiring decisions in case a suitable role becomes available. Another way to progress is by regularly updating your CV and job search profiles so you can be ready when potential employers are hiring someone new.

Progress is growth, setting goals, committing to them, and utilizing the skills of resilience and self-reflection to assist in pivoting and responding to the challenges of a competitive job market. When you fully understand your values, motivations, aspirations, and yourself as an employee, making realistic plans and goals is easier.

Progress is being open to reassessing and reviewing our job search goals, exploring ideas and options, and evolving those ideas to become realistic opportunities. You can progress towards your career goals in many ways, from updating your CV and job search profiles to getting coaching sessions with a career counselor or using online courses and tools for self-development.

This contributes to progress that results in authentic applications that express capabilities and suitability for the role and result in successful appointments to meaningful positions that align with values and career aspirations.

The recipe for progress is simple.

P : Planning, preparation, and pivoting

R : Reviewing, reassessing, and responding

O : Organising, orchestrating, and overcoming

G : Growth and goals

R : Resilience and responding

E : Exploration, evaluation, and evolution

S : Self-reflection and solution

Written By

Natalie Sims - Career Tree - Grow Your Future
Career Development Professional
NEC CDANZ Delivering Free Career Guidance to All New Zealanders

Do you believe failure is also progress?

What has your failures taught you about yourself?

What Is Pulling You More?

Your career growth depends on what pull you more

What Is Pulling You More?

This doodle resonates with me as there are two different yet realistic mindsets. Do we stay in the comfort zones of fear, doubt, and a fixed mindset? Making excuses as we don't want to push ourselves, take on new challenges for fear of failing? What will others think? Will we be letting down family and friends? If we have to study again, will we pass?

Do we suffer from imposter syndrome, believing those nagging doubts in our minds? We are not good enough; we can't do it! Do we stick to what we know as it's easier, stay in our comfort zone where it's safe and as far as we can go in our career?

Or do we open our minds, talk to a career guidance professional that can unlock our vision, purpose, and explore our aspirations? As humans, we function better if we enjoy what we do and, more importantly, have a purpose. Do we have a goal or vision of where we are heading, or are we happy to allow opportunities to unfold?

Aspiration is something you may have or perhaps still be developing. Our external influences can often affect what we can do or what we think is achievable; we will automatically put barriers up if something is uncomfortable or difficult. It's fine not to be sure about your purpose; our minds change and develop as we go through life, and experiences change our thinking. For me, trying new things, taking chances, and gaining experience are what's important. Some people's purpose may not be job satisfaction but a need to earn an acceptable wage to support their family. Education and training are often the key to expanding your earning potential and unlocking more job opportunities.

This links in nicely with a vision; it may be to move into another sector, earn more money, or for social interaction. Many people work past retirement for extra money and to work with others; this gives purpose, and their vision could be to keep going as long as they can. Vision is to look at where you are heading; it doesn't always have to be a promotion or more money; it could be as simple as work-life balance and being happy.

Some of my best career decisions have been to go for a job I think is out of my league. I have challenged my negative thinking, had courage in my skills, knowledge, and experience, and my ability to learn and develop. Sometimes it just takes a leap of faith and talking to others who can support you through the process and help you unpick your thoughts and empower you to go for it! I regularly talk to other career guidance professionals as I still have self-doubts; we spend so much of our lives working - it's important to be happy and have the balance that's right for us. We wouldn't leave a car without a service, so why do we not seek help for our careers?

Career isn't work; it's all-encompassing, affecting every aspect of our lives in which we need to find the work-life balance and financial stability that allows us to thrive.

Reflecting on the doodle, what is pulling you more right now?

Written By

Sally-Ann Monger
Careers Adviser | Registered Career Development Professional | Career Development Institute Member | BACVW Certified CV Writer | Supporting Neurodiversity & SEND

How can you cultivate a sense of being drawn towards your vision, aspirations, and future?

What Is in Your Career Success Folder?

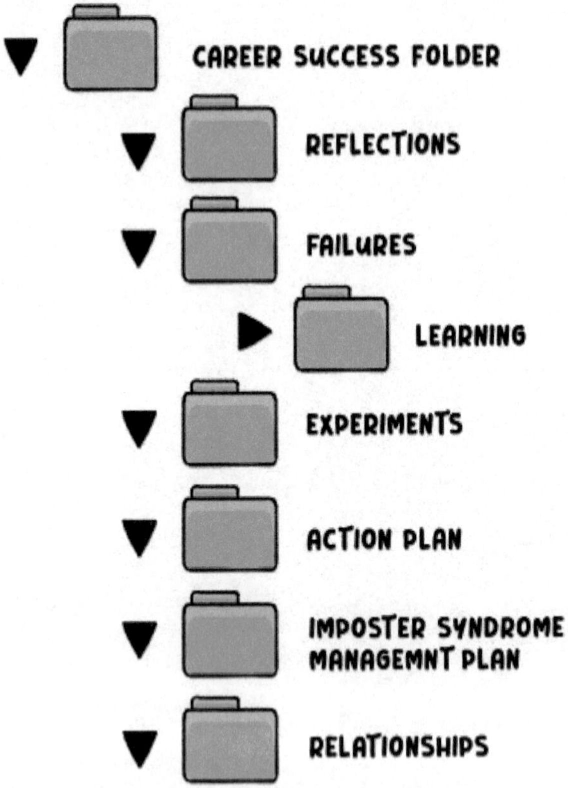

What Is in Your Career Success Folder?

There is no such thing as overnight success. Any path to success is more about the journey than the destination. The same can be said for our career success.

What does career success mean anyway?

The answer is whatever career success means to you. It means different things to each of us; you get to define it.

The challenge lies in the word "success". According to the Cambridge Dictionary, the word success is defined as "something that achieves positive results". Add the word "career" preceding "success" and we idealize in a false perspective of only those parts of our career that have gone well.

In fact, there's a richness which comes from the not-so-glamorous aspects of our career.

We often hear about careers defined in linear ways, such as career ladder or career path. We know our career is not straight. Instead, it is dynamic, customizable, and continually evolving. It is a wonderful mix of different start points and destinations which help to shape its success.

Everyone's career is their own journey. We all start from different places and our career journey takes us along a unique path. It is a beautiful blend of so many different elements all coming together to shape and frame our career as success. There is no right or wrong way to experience career success.

Behind any so-called career success is a beautiful blend of reflection, failures and learnings, experiments, action plans, imposter syndrome management plan, and relationships. We often learn the most about ourselves through looking back on our career. We also learn the value of those "bumps in the road" and come to appreciate their importance in our career journey.

My own career success journey has been filled with lots of experiments. Like the time I had graduated with a Certificate in International Travel and took a job reconciling airline tickets and chasing refunds for a travel wholesaler. I hated every minute of it and only lasted three months on the job. Whilst I could look at that time as a failure, I choose to look at it as a learning. It taught me just as much about what I enjoy doing as what I don't like doing.

I then pivoted and found a job as a retail travel agent and went on to spend three years in that organisation. I also earned my way to the third-highest seller in Australia. So what could have been considered a failure was reframed to be more of an experiment and learning which brought me closer to what I enjoy doing.

So everyone's career success is defined according to what's important to them. Regardless of how you define career success, the most important takeaway is to remember you are the CEO of your career and you get to shape your career success in a way most meaningful to you.

What is in your success folder? Write your reflections.

Written By

Jenny Hale
Passionate about all things remuneration and compensation related. In short, dedicated to paying people correctly and getting paid their worth.

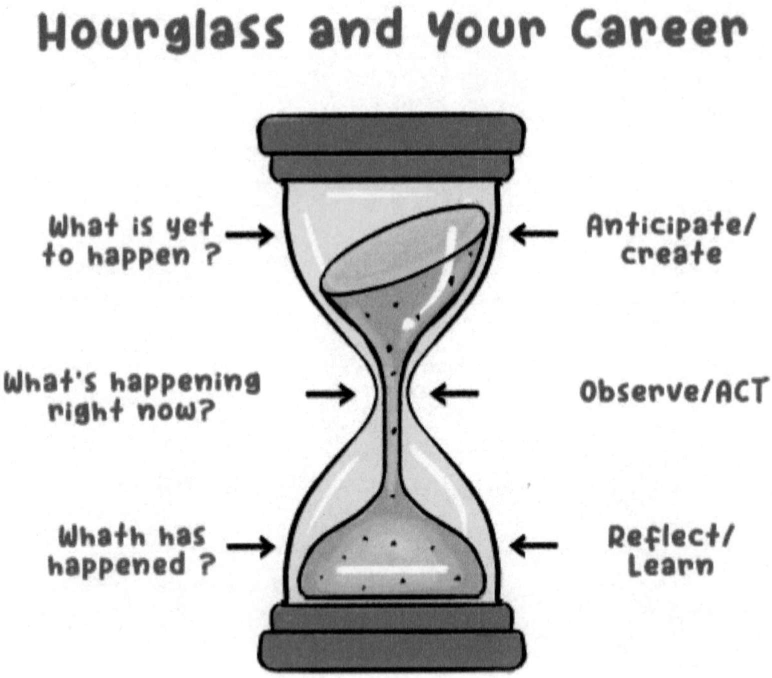
Hourglass and Your Career
What is yet to happen ?
Anticipate/ create
What's happening right now?
Observe/ACT
Whath has happened ?
Reflect/ Learn

Hourglass and Your Career

Who is responsible for your career?

- Your boss?
- Your company?
- The government?

Nope. You are.

Tony Robbins' 6 core human needs model suggests that all our actions are taken to meet our needs. We may or may not be able to name that need. We might even meet that need disgracefully or destructively. With a little reflection, we can name those needs and increase the regularity of which we meet them gracefully and constructively.

The six needs are:

1. Certainty: Our routines and habits help us to feel safe.
2. Uncertainty: Too much routine gets boring, and uncertainty brings excitement and adventure.
3. Belonging: It was once a matter of life and death, and it still feels better today than being alone.
4. Significance: Just being a part of the group isn't enough, and we want to feel special and/or important in the group.
5. Growth: You are either growing or dying.
6. Contribution: With your needs met, it is time to serve others.

Given the time you spend at work, it has a unique role in your life to provide the experiences to meet your needs. A career, your work, your combination of jobs are all reflections of the choices you have made. Can you identify the needs they have been meeting? Have you been meeting your needs disgracefully or constructively?

What combination of tasks and behaviours do you need to be valued in a work setting for your personal and career needs to be met?

To identify the tasks, you need to do more of, reflect over the last week and categorize all that you did in one of four categories:

- Your most valuable contribution
- What you love doing
- What you hate doing
- What can be delegated or automated

See what tasks you hate doing can be delegated and/or automated to make room for more of what you love and/or are your most valuable contributions.

Then reflect on your top three values. Give them a name, define them, identify examples, and give thought to how often you need to experience your values.

These two activities combined with the 6 core needs will have you well placed to take responsibility for being your best self and doing your best work.

Write your reflections about the doodle.

Written By

Brian Klindworth
Melbourne boy born to an American Dad and English Mum who co-parents and loves sport. He also works as a Career Coach and helps people to Be their best and Do their best work.

What do you think about the 6 core human needs model?

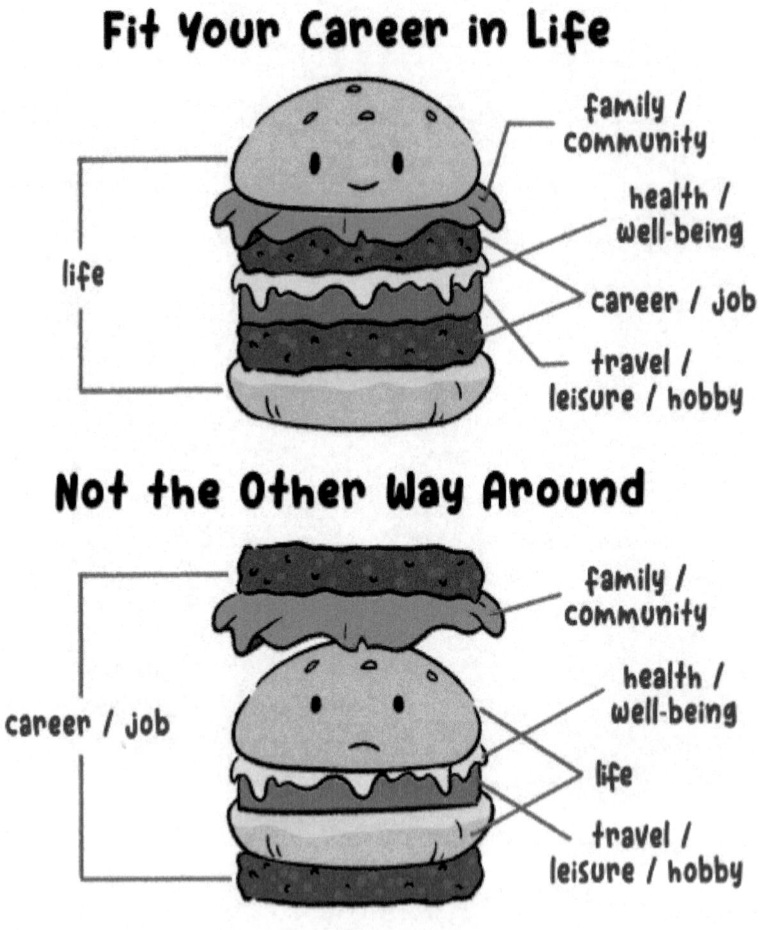
Fit Your Career in Life
family / community
health / well-being
life
career / job
travel / leisure / hobby
Not the Other Way Around
family / community
health / well-being
career / job
life
travel / leisure / hobby

Fit Your Career in Life, Not the Other Way Around.

We have heard many stories of people who, in our eyes as third-party observers, seem to have it all but feel discontented, and we wonder why they feel this way. This is because they don't have clarity about what makes up their life, which typically finds them running an endless and pointless race.

Each of us generally have about 6-10 areas in our lives that we consider important for a wholesome life. These usually include relationships, finance, health, fun or leisure, career, spirituality, contribution (e.g. to the community or the environment), and personal growth, which includes education. Living a fulfilled life means having each of these elements that you consider essential in your life working in tandem with each other.

Often, when people are not aware of the various elements that make up their life, they end up focusing on just one element that has to shoulder the weight of all the other elements. Unfortunately, this tends to lead to detrimental effects. For example, when a person focuses too much on their career without taking care of their health, the snowball effect from it may lead to taking time off work to recover. In the process, they could miss out on career opportunities, incur financial expenditures for said recovery instead of putting it into savings and investment, and lose time for building relationships, fun, leisure, or personal growth.

When you know what elements make up your life, going deeper into the aspects of each element will help you channel your time and energy appropriately to "have it all." Firstly, you will know what "all" constitutes. Secondly, you are able to recognise when you have it all and if you don't, specifically what is it that you're missing. Finally, because of that, you don't compare your "all" to others' because you recognize that your "all" is unique, and you take pride in that. Just like a Subway sandwich, you choose the fillings and condiments to make your own inimitable sandwich.

Hence, when you know what sandwich you want to have, you will find the ingredients that you'll need to make it. Bear in mind these points:

- We all have multiple meals in a day, week, month, and year. So, you're allowed to have a variety of sandwiches in the course of your life.
- Sometimes, some ingredients are harder to come by, and it'll test your patience, resilience, or resourcefulness to get them.

In other words, because you have clarity about what you want and need in your sandwich, you'll be able to know what ingredients to add or remove as you're making your sandwich, as well as know the right people around you whom you can ask to support you in putting together your sandwich.

Your sandwich is yours to make, and it's up to you to make it how you want it. Make a sandwich that fulfils you and not one that just fills you."

Where does your career fit in your "life sandwich" and how is this impacting the other areas in your life?

Written By

Adele Chee

Passionate for a world where everyone can create possibilities to live the life of their choice.

What is the impact that you want to have from your career?

What do you need to do differently with your career to achieve this impact?

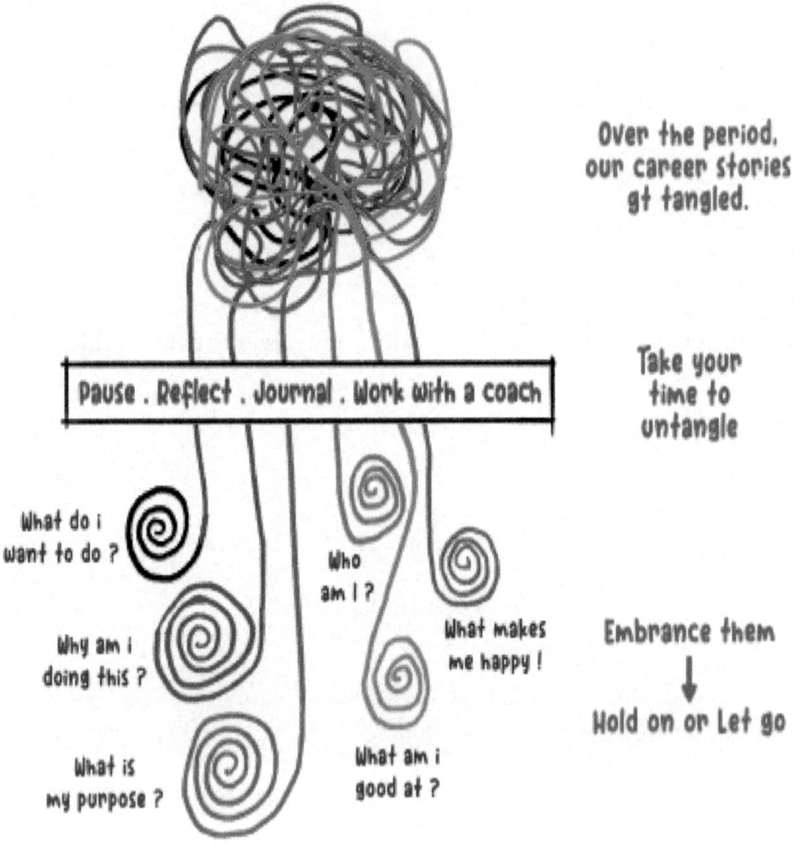
Over the period,
our career stories
gt tangled.
Pause . Reflect . Journal . Work with a coach
Take your
time to
untangle
What do i
want to do ?
Who
am I ?
What makes
me happy !
Why am i
doing this ?
What is
my purpose ?
What am i
good at ?
Embrance them
Hold on or Let go

Career Stories Are Tangled

Over a period, our career stories get tangled.

Life is busy. We can be so focused on getting on with things that we lose sight of whether we want to be doing those things! This is particularly true when it comes to our career.

We start a job, and we immerse ourselves in doing what needs to be done. We might be particularly good at doing what needs to be done and find ourselves with a promotion or two under our belts.

We keep on keeping on because that's what everybody does, right?

Or is it? What would happen if you took some time out to pause and reflect on your career? Give yourself an opportunity to unravel the spaghetti in your head and tease out exactly how you feel about your career.
Ask yourself:

- **What do I want to do?**

A deceptively simple question that so many find difficult to answer. If you had complete freedom and could spend your days doing anything at all, what would you do? Where would you direct your time, energy, and attention?

- **Why am I doing this?**

Is your choice of career an active or a passive choice? By that, I mean, do you pursue your current career path through choice or because you don't know what you would do instead? If it's the latter, then you are not alone. Very few of us spend time considering that first question of "what do I want?" which then leads us to keep on doing what we have always done.

- **What is my purpose?**

A big question. What do you believe in? What do you want to stand for? What is the legacy that you want to create through the work that you do?

- **Who am I?**

An even bigger question! You are a multi-faceted individual, and the work that you do is only one piece of the jigsaw of your identity. Brainstorm all of the roles that you hold e.g. father, brother, son, runner, swimmer, chef and consider where your career fits into your overall identity.

- **What am I good at?**

An even bigger question! You are a multi-faceted individual, and the work that you do is only one piece of the jigsaw of your identity. Brainstorm all of the roles that you hold e.g. father, brother, son, runner, swimmer, chef and consider where your career fits into your overall identity.

- **What makes me happy?**

Just because you are good at something doesn't mean it will make you happy. What lights you up? What causes are you passionate about? What work allows you to get into flow, where you can immerse yourself fully and hours melt away?

When you have the answers to these questions, you can then decide to carry on as you are or that it's time for a change and to do things differently.

The choice is yours.

What is my purpose?

Written By

Nicola Semple
Career and Confidence Coach and Host of The Career Confidence Podcast.

What do I want to do?

Why am I doing this?

Sometimes you need to zoom out
and look at how far you have come

Sometimes You Need to Zoom Out

SELF REFLECTION = SELF CARE

Modern-day life is so fast-paced. We're always so busy 'doing' and focused on targets, future goals, and "what's next?" But if we're always chasing the next thing, we miss the opportunity to enjoy the present moment and celebrate how far we have come. For me, this image brings a sense of calm in a sometimes chaotic world.

It reminds me of a conversation I recently had with my daughter. She was feeling a bit fed up that she couldn't get the hang of a new ukulele chord and wasn't making any progress. When we took a moment to zoom out and remember that only a few years ago she couldn't play anything, she suddenly realised how much she's achieved.

A similar comparison could be made by the way we look at our careers. We can often get preoccupied by the small day-to-day tasks and lose sight of the bigger picture. It can feel like small steps aren't getting us anywhere, but when we zoom out and look through a wider lens, we can see that the seemingly small steps have, in fact, been huge leaps collectively.

Similarly, when we have a bad day at work, it can feel all-consuming, but taking that all-important step back enables us to put things into perspective and recognize the progress we've made and how far we've come to get us to that point.

During our career journeys, it's inevitable that we will feel out of our comfort zone from time-to-time; starting a new job, taking on more responsibilities, venturing into self-employment, or working towards a new qualification. These things can feel scary, and we can feel out of our depth, but it's in these moments when it's even more important to zoom out and gain a better perspective of how far we've come. By looking back at our past achievements, and recognizing how much we have learnt and grown, we gain the courage to start something new because we realise we will be doing so with more experience and wisdom.

Self-reflection is an important life lesson. Taking a moment to step back and reflect on our successes is a form of self-care, and this simple picture is a perfect illustration of that. So much so that I printed it off to stick on the wall in my office! Whenever I'm starting to feel bogged down by a task and disheartened with a lack of progress, it encourages me to step into the hot air balloon in my mind and broaden my perspective. Thank you, Naishadh, for the gentle reminder.

We are all a work in progress, and it's so important to reflect on how far we have come, celebrate our achievements, and recognize that we are capable of further growth.

Take some time out. Sit in a quiet place and reflect on your career journey so far. What do you observe? Write your reflections.

Written By

Katherine Jennick
Registered Career Development Professional (RCDP) and Creator of the award winning What's Your Strength?® cards - empowering people to recognise, celebrate and share strengths

In the game of career,

are you a player or a spectator?

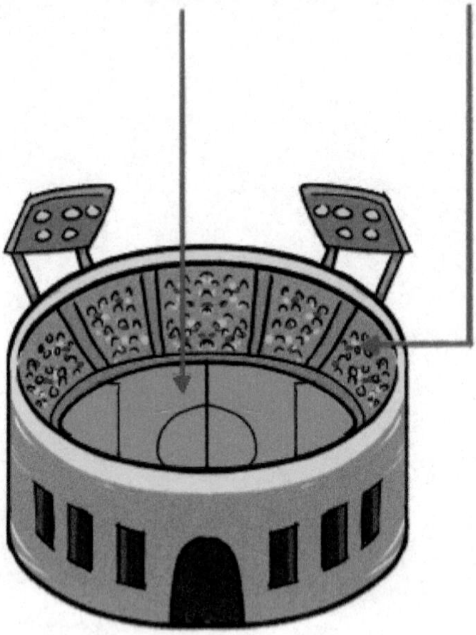

Are You a Player or Spectator?

Seeing this Doodle immediately reminded me of visiting the Colosseum in Rome and one of my favourite movies, Gladiator. After these two thoughts, Theodore Roosevelt's famous speech entitled "The Man in the Arena" came to mind.

"It is not the critic who counts; not the man who points out how the strong man stumbles, or where the doer of deeds could have done them better. The credit belongs to the man who is actually in the arena, whose face is marred by dust and sweat and blood; who strives valiantly; who errs, who comes short again and again, because there is no effort without error and shortcoming; but who does actually strive to do the deeds; who knows great enthusiasms, the great devotions; who spends himself in a worthy cause; who at the best knows in the end the triumph of high achievement, and who at the worst, if he fails, at least fails while daring greatly, so that his place shall never be with those cold and timid souls who neither know victory nor defeat."

How does this relate to the game of a career?

I think it goes to the heart of how we see our careers, whether we see ourselves as active participants who are there to play or spectators who are there to watch. To be playing in the arena is to bring intention, purpose, and passion to our career. It's to ask the questions:

- What is my calling and purpose at work?
- How am I contributing my strengths?
- What do I care about most deeply?
- How do I want to serve?

It's also asking ourselves the brave questions:

- Why am I not thriving here?
- Where can I be most myself?
- Who am I being at work?

And when the answers are not aligned with who we are or who we want to be in the world – it's time to make a career change. All these questions, the exploration, the reflections, and discovery are active play. It's us choosing to play in the arena. It's not standing or sitting in seats eating snacks, cheering, or maybe throwing stones, calling out insults, booing or jeering.

It's us playing through hardship, disappointment, rejections, demotions, redundancies, terminations, and average performance reviews. It's also us actively playing through promotions, glowing feedback, achievements, wins, connection, and belonging.

For better and worse, we want to be in the career arena playing even if we are getting our butts kicked. Because one thing is for sure, we can't play as spectators. We can only watch.

To determine whether you are a player or a spectator in the context of your career game, ask yourself the following questions:

1. Am I taking ownership of my career and making deliberate choices to advance my goals?
2. Am I actively seeking out opportunities to learn and grow in my profession?
3. Do I have a clear vision and goals for my career, and am I taking steps to achieve them?
4. Am I being proactive in making strategic moves to advance my career, or am I waiting for opportunities to come to me?
5. Am I taking risks and making calculated decisions to improve my career prospects, or am I playing it safe and staying in my comfort zone?

Written By

Jasmine Malki
Learning designer, Facilitator and Coach. Helping organisations nurture loving workplaces so people belong and make a lasting contribution to our world through their work.

Career Agility

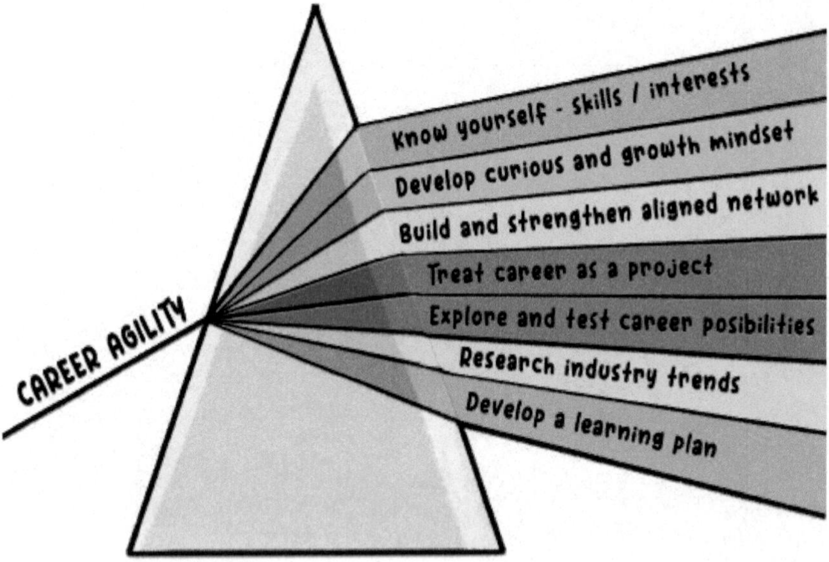

Career Agility

I really like this Doodle, not least of all because it reminds me of the album cover to one of the most iconic records ever sold; Pink Floyd's Dark Side of the Moon. Oh yes, and the refraction of light lessons we toiled through in Year 8 Science.

When I started my career journey, 5-10 years at a company demonstrated loyalty, dedication, and was seen as a positive on someone's CV, even if they dared to look for a new job, which they rarely did unless retrenched. In larger companies, the lure of 'long service leave' was just too tempting to resist.

Fast forward 30 years, anything more than 3 years in a company and you can often be viewed as stale, lacking ambition, and settled in a 'job' not a career.

My own 'career' has encompassed IT, recruitment, real estate, dental, construction, recycling, and commercial cleaning – about as diverse as you can get. Some of it through choice and some through necessity, as business dropped off in one and new opportunities arose in others.

The one thing I always hold, though, is a keenness to connect, a willingness to learn, a curiosity to find out more, and an interest in finding out where the next 'interesting' dollar can be earned. You see, earning money is but a small, but important, part of the decision-making process, and we all know money doesn't bring happiness (we are told that often enough, anyway).

OK, so you may have a specific degree that allows you to follow your dream and work in one industry for your whole life – fantastic, and I applaud you. For the rest of us, however, industry changes, demand drops off for certain occupations, whether those jobs are sent overseas or just not required anymore through automation and the like. It is acknowledging how to use those 'transferable' skills and how they can be utilized in a new industry.

Your time in the workforce is the same as everyone else's pretty much; unless you die, work for the government, or hit on that billion-dollar idea, in which case your time may be shorter. However, how you experience that time can go quickly or feel like an eternity. Better for it to go quickly, and as they say, "time flies when you are having fun." That applies to the workforce as much as any other situation.

Make a difference, or not. Do what you love, and if not, what you can enjoy for the money. And work to live. You can have many jobs but only one life, so you may as well make the most of it."

To determine if you have career agility, which refers to the ability to adapt and thrive in a constantly changing work environment, you can ask yourself the following questions:

1. Am I willing to take on new challenges and learn new skills?
2. Do I actively seek out feedback and opportunities for growth and development?
3. Am I comfortable with change and able to adapt quickly to new situations?
4. Do I have a diverse network of professional contacts and seek out opportunities to connect with others?
5. Am I comfortable with ambiguity and able to navigate uncertain situations?

Written By

Alex Barritt
Business Development Manager & Relationship Builder. Still living in Melbourne, following a 2 week holiday from the UK in November 2000.

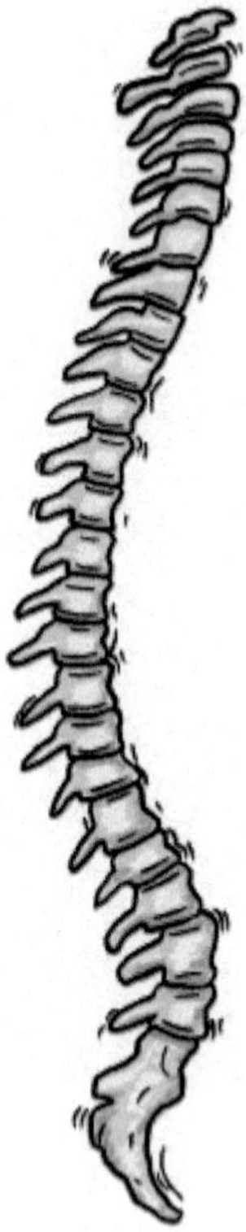

career values are
like a
spinal cord.

A minor
misalignment
can cause
career-ache.

Career Values Are Like a Spinal Cord. A Minor Misalignment Can Cause Career-Ache

Career values are like a spinal cord. A minor misalignment can cause career ache.

This doodle reminds me of a little nagging feeling or small "pain" that, if not addressed, gets worse and has the potential to spread and impact other areas of our lives, just like back pain could.

I learned about career values through working. Early in my career, I worked for a well-regarded company. I was pinching myself and felt "successful" being in such lovely surroundings; however, this did not last. The culture was intensely competitive, working very long hours was normal, and I was acutely aware of my place at the bottom of a very hierarchical structure. While many staff enjoyed and thrived in this environment and continue to do so, it was not for me. I felt uncomfortable.

In hindsight, this is when my career values developed. I moved to another organisation that was a much better fit for me and thrived.

-

Meaningful work matters, though what is meaningful to one person is not to another. What we value in our careers/work is likely to change over time.

While most of us can and do compromise our values to some extent in exchange for valuable experience, a much-needed job, CV value, or promotional opportunity – this "misalignment" is likely to cause us career ache over time.

Some examples of career values in action:

- Client A had been with her current employer for 14 months and is enjoying her role. She had been offered a promotion but declined as she had observed her new manager speaking disparagingly and inappropriately about two of her valued colleagues in an open area. She has since moved to another employer.
- Client B is a real estate professional. He loves his work and has been with his employer for 10 years. He no longer values the prize. Considering what he wants out of the next stage of his career/life, he moved to a sales/marketing role with a B corporation, reflecting his developing interest in sustainable

practices. He has taken a pay cut but is working regular hours and is now able to spend more time with his young family.

Reflect on your career values – there are plenty of good tools online to help you with this. Be realistic and decide what's negotiable and what's not.

Identify a prospective employer's values by doing your due diligence. What is their mission statement, and how do their internal programs/processes genuinely support this? Read their latest press releases, annual report summary, and social media posts. What do they look for in staff? Who is on their board/leadership team, and what do they stand for? Don't be afraid to ask questions at an interview related to your top values, for example, if professional development is important to you, ask the company for more information about theirs. Consider to what extent your career values align with your prospective employer's. In my experience, the more aligned your work is to your career values, the better the outcome.

What are your career values?

Written By

Helen Green CDAA, RPCDP
Careers Coach & Careers Feature Writer
Director, Career Confident.
www.careerconfident.com.au

How do you keep your career aligned with the values?

Our Careers Grow at Different Speeds – and That's Okay.

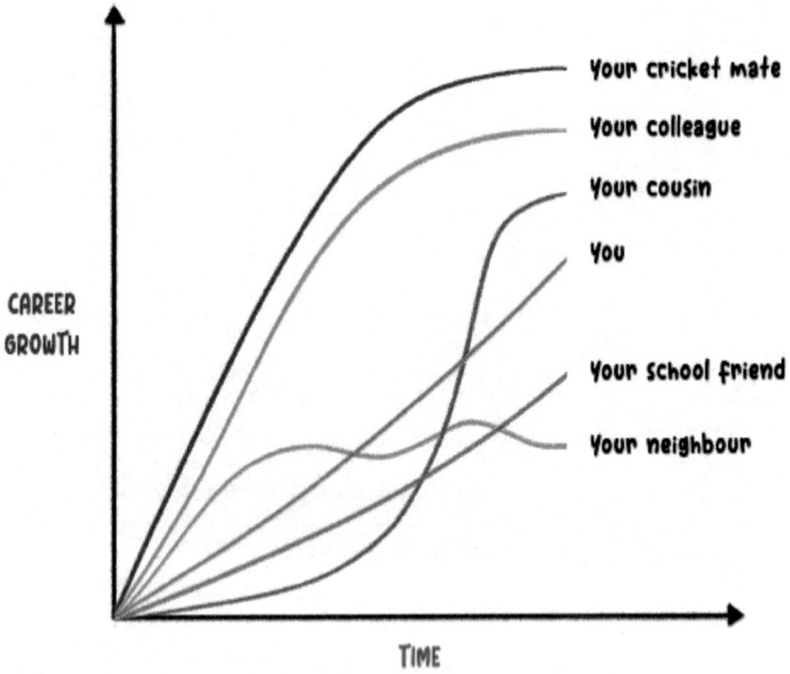

Our careers grow at different speeds - and that's okay.

There are seasons when we sprint - when we get the juicy assignment, hit the next rank, get the promotion, or get elevated to management.

There are seasons when we plateau, when nothing exciting happens, and we begin to doubt our abilities and worry that we are falling behind.

It has been said that comparison is the thief of joy.

It is when we compare ourselves to others that we start to judge ourselves and others, saying things like "they are better than" and "I am less than".

We look at our more successful colleagues' possessions, families, professional titles, appearances, and we make up stories about them.

Comparison sparks envy - when we are busy comparing and judging, we look at ourselves and start to feel inadequate, then we go into a vicious loop of berating ourselves mentally for not being good enough.

It is almost like we have a human compulsion to fit everyone - including ourselves - into a neat little box that we can label and understand, so we know where everyone belongs in the bigger picture.

But life is not as tidy and linear and predictable as we would like, and appearances are deceiving.

There are seasons of shedding - when leaves change color and fall.

Seasons of stillness and seeming inactivity - when trees stand white and bare in winter.

There are seasons of immense growth - when flowers blossom, bees gather to feast, and fruit trees produce a joyful harvest.

Everything in nature respects the universal laws of change, the cycle of ebb and flow, of growth and stagnation, of life and death.

Let's take a leaf from Life and allow ourselves to experience cycles and seasons in our careers, without making it a reflection of our personal self-worth and our competency and capability.

We are much more than the jobs we have and where we fit in the hierarchy of prestigious professions.

Whether you are a tradie, a student, an IT analyst, a business owner, or an accountant, you cannot demand that you will experience only upward progression and success and avoid failures and setbacks by doing all the right things and making all the right moves.

Life is an opportunity to keep evolving and innovating and transforming into something better, and there are many ways to experience this.

When you are experiencing a slow season and seemingly making no progress in your career, or wondering if you are in the right career, look for the hidden lessons and blessings, and focus on what and who you are grateful for.

When everything is going your way in your career and people are congratulating you on your good fortune, give thanks, stay humble, and look at how else you can grow and give back to others.

In the larger scheme of things, how far we get in our careers is but one snapshot among many in a long and well-lived life.

When we look back on our lives, it is our relationships that we prize the most – who we love, who loves us, fun times and adventures, laughter and music and art and nature and delicious food, and the priceless memories of times spent with loved ones.

Written By

Serena Low
Empowering Quiet Achievers to grow into Quiet Warriors.

Let's accept, we all compare our career with everyone's careers. How has it impacted your career?

What strategies have you developed to lessen the impact?

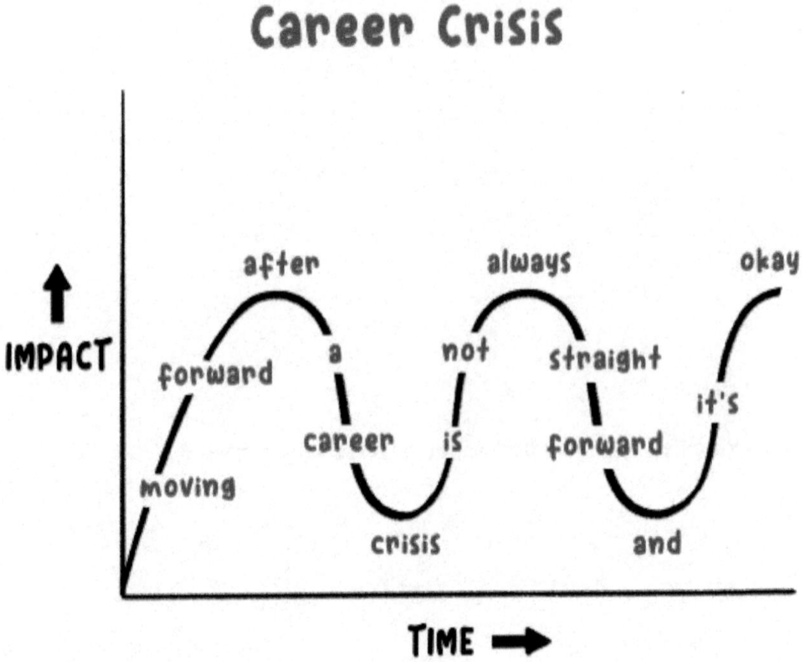
Career Crisis
IMPACT
TIME
moving
forward
after
a
career
crisis
is
not
always
straight
forward
and
it's
okay

Career Crisis

Career crises are something that most people encounter during their career. It could be missing out on your dream job, a bad boss, being bullied, being made redundant or fired, or suffering an illness. It could also be a career crisis where you realise that you need to change your career.

How the career crisis impacts you, and the time required to move forward and recover, depends on many factors. These include the severity of the crisis, openness to change, your prior career planning and preparedness, personal resilience, support available to you, and the actions you take to move on.

A career crisis is often a form of change. There are two types of change: change that we create ourselves and change that is imposed on us by others. Most human beings prefer to stay in their comfort zone and try to avoid change, especially change we didn't choose. However, career change is inevitable, and we need to learn to manage it. The only job or career security we have is that which we create for ourselves, through our self-efficacy, employability, career planning with plans B and C (or more), and practicing resilience.

It can be very upsetting when a career crisis happens to us, especially when it takes us out of our comfort zone and impacts our income. It takes time to adjust to the new situation, often with many ups and downs before we find a positive way forward.

This doodle reminds me of Kubler-Ross's Change Curve, which aligns with her original Stages of Grief model, because we tend to go through similar emotions. These include Shock, Denial, Frustration/Anger, Bargaining, Depression, Experimenting, Decision Making, and Integration/Acceptance.
This model shows us that we will have ups and downs (maybe even two steps

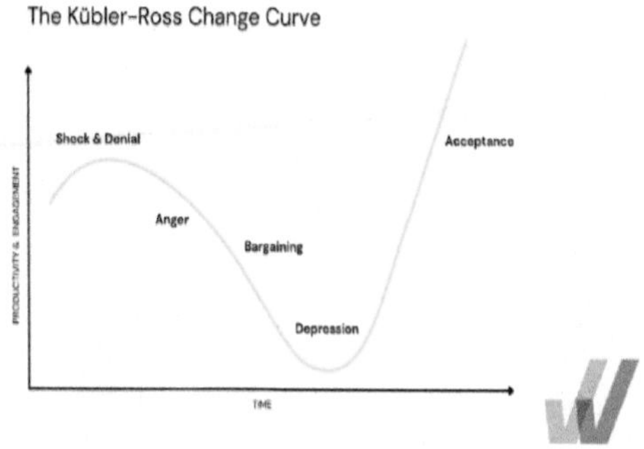

Image Credit: https://whatfix.com/blog/kubler-ross-change-curve/

forward and one step back), our responses to change are not linear, it will take time, and that's ok.

The key is to be kind to ourselves, not to blame ourselves for the situation, and seek help when we are stuck. It is important to take advantage of professional support, including EAP counselling, working with a career coach, or outplacement services.

ADKAR is another model that can help us deal with imposed or chosen career change, which stands for Awareness, Desire, Knowledge, Ability, and Reinforcement.

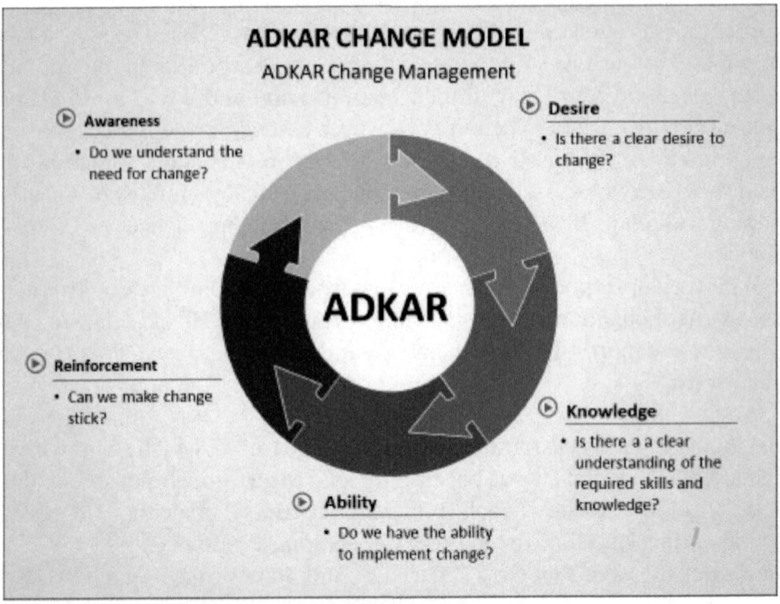

Image Credit:
https://www.techno-pm.com/2020/11/adkar-model-change-competency-assessment.html

Written By

Melita Long, Careers on Purpose
Career & Executive Coach, LinkedIn & Resume Writer, 20 years helping mid-career professionals identify and achieve their ideal career.

This model encourages us to be aware of why the change has occurred, what we can learn from it, be clear on our new direction, gain the knowledge, skills, and ability we need to take us forward, and use reinforcement to make it stick. This is where having a support network to help you on your path can make a positive impact.

If you are going through a career crisis, be kind to yourself, seek support, find the positives, and give yourself time.

In my career coaching experience, within 6 months or less, 90% of clients realised that their redundancy, job loss, or career change was a blessing in disguise, and most people end up much better off.

What did you learn about yourself from the experience?

Work-Life Balance vs. Work-Life Blend
Work
Relationships / Family
Hobbies / Passions
Side Hustle
Self - Care
Voulteering
Health
Travel / Leisure
Try until you like the blend

Tried Work-Life Balance? Now, Try Work-Life Blend

I hate cooking, or rather, the thought that a woman's life revolves around the kitchen. There is so much more that women are capable of doing. They are reaching for the stars, breaking glass ceilings, and going into jobs that were once considered the exclusive domain of men. Yet, women also find themselves trapped with the image of being a nurturer. That's the first thought this image and its wording evoked in me.

I got trapped into thinking that work-life balance is only about women, and it's only about how they feel when they have to juggle far more than men. It is stereotyping. Years of conditioning have made our minds automatically associate the kitchen and its varied appliances with women.

In the same way, we assume that everything we do professionally is "work" and that the rest of things come under "life" (family, personal goals, hobbies) as we see or make of it. Both of them are distinct and at opposite ends of the spectrum. When one end is up, the other end is down, and only a fine balance can help one maintain continuity.

Alas, life is not always a fine balance. It is a wonderful mix of ups and downs, of the trivial and the important, of the mundane and the critical.

What if one were to prioritize "life" over "work"? What if the things that really consume one are in the "life" area and do not necessarily fall under the "work" bucket? Would life-work balance then be different? Would the end result be different? **Imagine this world.**

But what if we were to not focus on the balance at all? Instead, what if we blended both "work" and "life"? How would our lives change then? **Imagine this world.**

The blended mix offers limitless possibilities. One day extra at work today and the next time, less so that you can follow your passion outside work. There is no question of compromise or sacrifice, or one at the cost of the other. **Imagine this world.**

The seamless act of flowing through the quadrants of "work" and "life" based pursuits can open new vistas for our growth. What is important is the right mix and the right blend, just like for any cooking wherein it is the right amount of ingredients that play a big role in how delicious the end product is going to be.

Ask yourself what a good life looks like for you, what it means to you. What do you need to put in that blender for things to work out? What if you begin by articulating the end goal first... say, wanting a fulfilling and content life? What ingredients would go into making the right mix for this end goal? What would determine the right taste?

John Coleman, co-author of Passion & Purpose: Stories from the Best and Brightest Young Business Leaders, defines "work" as anything we **have** to do and "life" as anything we **want** to do. How does a blend of this world sound to you? **Imagine this world.**

The work-life blend offers many different worlds. Which one do you want to imagine?

Written By

Sarita Bahl
ICF Certified Coach (ACC) &
EMCC Accredited Sr Practitioner
specializing in career transition, inner
engineering and life issues.

Tried Work-Life Balance? Now, Try Work-Life Blend

I have often been asked, ***"Vineti, how do you balance work and life so well?"*** Can one have it all? Does work-life balance exist, and is it possible to have a balance after all?

Let's start with understanding what work-life balance is. It is the ability to manage one's professional and personal life in a way that allows for productivity, fulfillment, and overall well-being. So here is my take on actual work-life balance or blend.

I have to be honest when Naishadh asked me to submit a write-up. I loved the idea of choosing to have a blend of entire work and life because every time I heard the words balancing, I always got the visual of me standing on a string with a balancing stick, where on one side of the stick is the heaviness of work and on the other side, my personal life pulling me. Now that is a very stressful visual! And I am sure no one wants that!

What a work-life blend means to me is to have enough energy and opportunity to spend time with family and friends, pursue hobbies, perform at work, and have time for yourself. For that, it is necessary to draw a line sometimes. At the same time, it means constantly prioritizing and reassessing professional and personal needs, making conscious choices about where to spend more energy and time, and being disciplined about it.

So, is it all that simple, as said? No, not really, but what makes it doable is taking back control of your choices and being smart about it. I have a process where every morning, I look at what is on today and what activities or actions I must do to make myself feel fulfilled when I finish for the day. It can be completing a presentation, completing my 10,000 steps, and committing to spend time with family and friends. To do this, I often try to blend things like taking kids swimming so that while the kids do their classes, I can complete my fitness goal!

I don't for a minute believe that I am a superwoman (which I have occasionally been called); far from super anything; however, being aware of personal and professional boundaries and being able to enforce them without hesitation is undoubtedly a superpower I have cultivated through practice. So, saying no to activities when you feel your personal or emotional energy is depleting is an essential aspect of the blend. Reenergizing yourself through activities that light your fire within is equally important. I often re-energize by simply being alone, listening to music or going for a walk, and I am grateful that my support system, my near and dear ones, understand and support that. So make time for yourself, take small breaks, and do activities that fill your glass because guess what? You cannot share from an empty glass!

This way, I am not stressing about the balancing act but making a blend of ingredients where each ingredient can change depending on the day's theme. Another essential skill that sometimes makes a hectic day somewhat manageable is being flexible, so I am always ready for a surprise that a day can throw at me, usually a call from school for a pick-up. All that means is looking at the list of to-do and reprioritizing! NO PRESSURE to get the perfect mix or balancing act on a string. Adapt, as the day goes.

This strategy has created a blend of work and life for me that has helped me manage stress, develop healthier relationships, and be more successful in my professional and personal life.

What is your current work-life blend made of?

Written By

Vineti Anand
Co-Founder and Director of APOC
Creating culturally intelligent leaders.

What can you add or remove from the blend?

Career Advice
Hacks to find dream job in less than 30 days

Career Advice or How to Get a Job in 30 Days

YOUR LIFE, YOUR CHOICE

Work and workplaces are rapidly changing. These changes are permanent and profound, and they are increasingly shaping career decisions. Employers are looking for ways to enhance performance, increase profits, become more agile and lean, while employees are seeking increased flexibility and work-life balance. Wage is no longer the determining factor in career choice, and employees are choosing lifestyle options, which in turn is shaping how work and working conditions are conceptualised. Choice is increasingly valued.

1. **Career vs. Job:** As opportunities and needs are rapidly changing, so too is our view of employment. Traditionally, the majority of people preferred the security, simplicity, and consistency of being an employee. Careers were promoted as lifelong, and being unemployed was seen as a failure and a cost to the community. Jobs were traditionally seen as a 'means to an end' for earning money. Career advice was youth-centred, believing that getting people into a lifelong career was 'better' than moving from job to job. Now, the concept of career embraces all forms of income-generating employment activities. Gigs, portfolio, itinerant work, all are options. The new norm is to become entrepreneurial, innovative and creative in the way that 'working' better meets lifestyle choices.
2. **Employee vs. Employer:** Since the advent of IR4.0, and especially since the pandemic, people have increasingly become entrepreneurial (creative & innovative) in their lifestyle choices. Increasingly, self-marketing and job searching include developing proposals and presenting ideas, which, in fact, create opportunities for paid engagement. Entrepreneurship should not be confused with enterprise (business). Entrepreneurs look for and communicate opportunities and solutions not previously seen. Certainly, paralleling entrepreneurship is the growth of small businesses. ABN registrations have increased significantly since the global financial crisis of the 1990s, escalating again during the pandemic. People making a career change later in life typically seek or create opportunities that will give them better lifestyle and work flexibility. Self-employment is one option to achieve these goals.

3. **Chance vs. Choice:** Australia, as in other parts of the world, has experienced unprecedented natural disasters. We went from drought to fires to flooding. Each of these events reminds us that governments (and employers) are not able to support people effectively. Those who have experienced sudden changes in their careers also know that systems are not able to effectively support them. Leaving life to chance seems increasingly problematic. We better understand that happiness and success are more likely to come because of self-management, initiative, creativity, and innovative, decisive action. Self-discovery and self-management are critical mindsets and capabilities in achieving goals.
4. **Life Hacks vs. Career Advice:** Self-management does not mean 'going it alone.' It ought not to be a solitary pursuit. We have also learned that collaborative practices always bring better results. Interestingly, we think nothing of seeking and paying for advice or guidance if we are making an investment, buying a house, buying a car, or planning a holiday. Generally, people, however, do not consider gaining professional career advice. The queue is short, pockets are deep, and arms are short. Yet when sought, the dividends/returns/ benefits are high. Your life is yours. It is the most important life you will have. Invest wisely.

Written By

Allan Gatebny
Associated Career Professional International Enabling happier lives through career, life-design & leadership coaching & training.

Write your reflections on the sketch.

Meaning of Work
What do you do?
Why do you do what you do?

Meaning of Work

Everywhere you look, you will see people working, making coffees, fixing roads, or busily doing their thing - whatever it may be. What is less obvious, however, is what sits below the waterline: their motivations. Not only can these be vastly different for each unique individual, but people's expectations of work - the core reason that drives them - are also undergoing some fairly monumental shifts.

In his fascinating book, What Makes Us Tick (2010), Australian social researcher Hugh Mackay outlines the following desires that can help us make better sense of who we are and why we do what we do:

1. The desire to be taken seriously
2. The desire for "my place"
3. The desire for something to believe in
4. The desire to connect
5. The desire to be useful
6. The desire to belong
7. The desire for more
8. The desire for control
9. The desire for something to happen
10. The desire for love

Interestingly, Mackay begins his book with a clear assertion that it is a Western myth that we are fundamentally rational beings, stating that "we are ruled more by the heart than the head." That, in itself, should give us pause for thought in terms of the advice we give and seek and the process by which we expect to arrive at a good decision.

Underlying many of Mackay's observations is the clear sense that we are tribal in nature, or pack animals if you prefer. We crave belonging, or in the language of Brené Brown, we are wired for connection. This is evident in recent research by Reventure that found up to 40% of Australians feel lonely at work, with knock-on impacts relating to their wellbeing and productivity. A hundred years ago, it would be rare to find the key driver behind employment choice being friendship and connection, but 21st-century workers often have their basic survival needs (water, food, shelter, clothing) amply met and are now looking for more.

Even the pursuit of happiness is being questioned as the ultimate goal, despite so many parents stating outright that it is what they seek for their children (i.e., "I just want them to be happy"). In contrast, Emily Esfahani Smith presents a compelling case for the pursuit of a meaningful life as being ultimately more fulfilling and, therefore, desirable. And what are her '4 pillars' that together uphold this mode of existence?

1. Belonging: connection to one another and to the community
2. Purpose: being intentional about making a positive contribution to the world
3. Storytelling: making sense of our experience by way of a positive, redemptive narrative

4. Transcendence: the humbling and awe-inspiring belief that there is more to life in the universe than mere stardust and random chance

Whether you are struggling to understand the behaviour of another person or facing options and wrestling to make a 'clear-headed' decision, it might be a good idea to take some time to look below the waterline and consider the desires, drivers, and ultimate 'why' that might quietly and powerfully be influencing the things you can more easily observe. Get to know yourself a bit better and step up your level of curiosity in seeking to better know others.

You might just find yourself living more empathetically, patiently, and purposefully as a result!

Written By

Claire Harvey
Career Coach at Echo Coaching, with an emerging focus on ecological and climate conscious coaching and supporting future-fit leaders.

Meaning of Work

The top of an iceberg, the visible part, is one-eighth of the whole. Seven-eighths of an iceberg, the most powerful section, is hidden beneath the water, creating stability, ballast. The Titanic, possibly the most famous iceberg casualty of all time, was brought undone by the unseen ice below the water. Racing the ship along through calm conditions, the captain believed his crew would spot icebergs in time to avert catastrophe. He underestimated the power of what could not be seen.

Events and actions are the visible part of our lives and careers. Like the top of an iceberg, our behaviours are a small part of the whole picture. Beneath the surface, anchoring the choices we make, are the stories, experiences, systems, structures, and values that make us who we are. We come to know the values of others and ourselves through actions. To paraphrase Nietzsche, if we understand our values, our 'why,' it is possible to find our 'how.'

With awareness of our values, we are better able to figure out why a particular comment or conversation at work feels so important or how it is that our dream job is starting to feel like a nightmare. Stories are excellent tools, helping to uncover the values hidden below the surface of our lives. There are remembered occasions that hold enduring importance as we journey through our career. Recalling rewarding, important, impactful, powerful events allow us to explore the experiences we value most. Often our most cherished stories have elements in common and help clarify what matters most to us. Our collected treasures illustrate our 'why.'

Career stories are filled with the people we meet along the way. These characters may take on roles as a mentor, protagonist, changemaker, antagonist, or foil. By choice or unconsciously, we learn from and imitate the people who impact our journey. In recalling memorable people from our career and life experiences and considering the qualities we admire or dislike from their example, we can better appreciate the traits and values we hold dear. Colleagues and friends will attest to the qualities they witness in us.

The rate of change and development in today's world of work means linear employment pathways and clear voyages are becoming rare. It is important to explore what we cannot see as well as what is visible to hone our navigation skills. Journey well!

Ask the following questions to yourself.

---

1. What values are most important to me? Why are these values important to me?
2. What are my strengths and skills? How can I use these to make a positive impact in the world?
3. What do I enjoy doing the most? What brings me the greatest joy and fulfillment?
4. What do I want to be remembered for? What impact do I want to have on the world?
5. What problems or challenges do I care deeply about solving? Why are these issues important to me?
6. What have been some of the most meaningful experiences in my life? What made them meaningful?
7. Who are the people I admire and why do I admire them? What qualities do they embody that I aspire to?
8. What is my unique contribution to the world? What do I have to offer that no one else does?

Written By

Leigh Pickstone
Career Development Practitioner,
Facilitator, and Teacher
Empowering people to successfully
navigate their career journey.

Leaning Against the Right Wall

"If the ladder is not leaning against the right wall,
every step we take just gets us to the wrong place faster."

- Stephen R. Covey

Leaning Against the Right Wall

I believe that the mid-life crisis suffers from some unfortunate reputational damage. We know the trope within popular culture, often involving a man leaving his devoted family for a younger woman and a sports car. The disservice that such stereotypes bring is a failure to take a good crisis sufficiently seriously, and to milk them for all they're worth. Whether it is traditional spirituality or modern psychotherapy, the idea that adults often reach a point in their lives where they feel the overwhelming need to reassess some fairly basic assumptions about who they are, how they're wired, and what they ultimately want out of life is a fairly universal theme. Like a snake shedding its skin or a butterfly going through a metamorphosis, abrupt and rather radical life changes can be a real thing. This is especially the case for those who have grown up to be highly compliant in nature, never challenging or questioning the status quo, and dutifully fulfilling the scripts that others have carefully written for them. It might be gradual, or sudden, but a day may come when the solid earth of what they've always thought they've known about life and the universe falls away, and everything is suddenly up for re-examination.

I recall a story of a retail worker who sold and installed stereo systems in cars. He speaks of enjoying spending time with a father-son customer duo, and the great excitement they exuded in selecting a sound system to go in the nearly-18-year-old's brand-new car. The sound system of choice was put on order, and some time passed. And then the father phoned to cancel the order, as his son had tragically died in an accident. This story shook this particular salesman to the core. He questioned the fragility of his own existence, and whether he was making the most of his own opportunity to truly live. That encounter, and the tough existential questions that followed, led him to quit his job and enroll in a psychology degree. I had the good fortune of meeting him years later when he was working as a clinical psychologist, still telling the story of what shook up his world as he'd known it.

The challenge is, for those of us who care deeply for others (and who might even sense that someone dear to us is on their own road to unfulfillment, if not ruin), is that a good crisis is one that we need to recognize, accept, and come to embrace for ourselves. It is not a task that can be necessarily compelled for another or conveniently subcontracted out. Just like forcibly removing a butterfly from its cocoon before it's ready will cause damage - if not death, tough and patient love often means walking alongside a person in crisis, providing a sufficiently supportive and safe space that allows a crisis to break, to blossom, and to eventually bear fruit, all in its own good time. Those of us who have been through various crises of our own can, in such seasons, be beacons of hope. We offer living proof that not only is there life on the other side of crisis, sometimes it's a better, richer, fuller kind of life! A life that is no longer characterized by the 'safety' of pain avoidance and the skillful circumvention of potential disaster, but instead one that exudes the courageous embrace of risk and new adventure, deeper joy, and an extraordinary gratitude for the incredible gift of simply being alive.

"The bad news is you're falling through the air, nothing to hang on to, no parachute. The good news is, there's no ground."

—Chögyam Trungpa

Reflect on this question and write your reflections. Are you leaning against the right wall?

____

____

____

____

____

____

____

Written By

Claire Harvey
Career Coach at Echo Coaching, with an emerging focus on ecological and climate conscious coaching and supporting future-fit leaders.

Boost Your Career Confidence

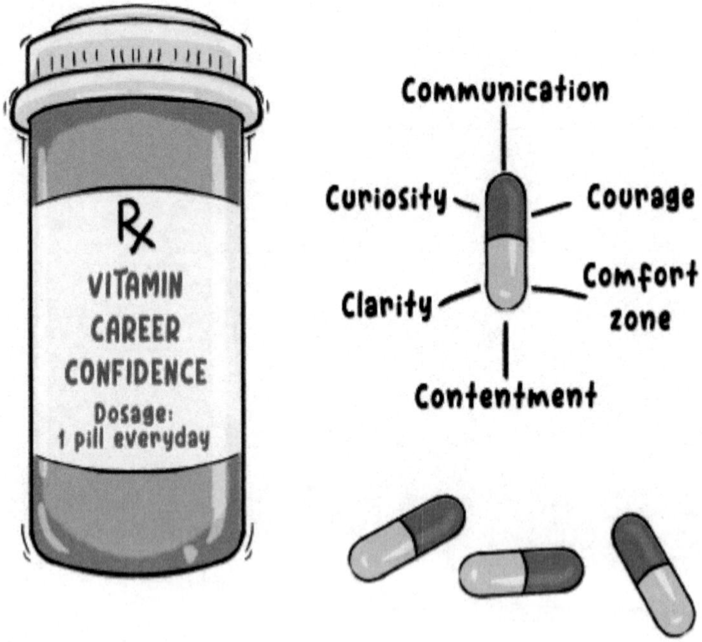

Boost Your Career Confidence

Twenty-five years ago, I managed a large pharmacy, including a methadone clinic that was open 14 hours a day. Half of my staff were young people either at school or university. During 2000, the pharmacy was held up several times by two male methadone patients, wearing masks and brandishing large knives. The holdups had a devastating effect on the lives of our team – particularly our young team members. It had a devastating effect on me: I left the world of pharmacy and vowed never to be in a position where I managed people again.

I look back now and wonder how I could have supported these young people differently as they were jettisoned from their comfort zone. How could I have instilled them with resilience? How could I have helped them communicate in order to process the trauma? How could I have given them (and myself) the strength and skills to return to this place of work?

Post-pharmacy, I returned to my family farm and, as fate would have it, whatever I did I found myself surrounded by young people. I resolved, this time, to spend my next career seeking out the best in the world to build their grit and resilience, and every day I am awed as they build their courage muscles.
Your career, and life, will not always go as planned, and gaining career confidence means equipping yourself with the skills to navigate troubled waters. It may be as simple as learning how to manage difficult conversations in order to achieve clarity and resolve pain points. It may be as major as dealing with a man brandishing a knife.
Before the hardships arrive, devote as much time to learning the soft skills of employment as you do to the practicalities of your job. Network with colleagues, seek mentors, develop skills, learn from experts, and build your self-belief. This is not a quick fix – or as simple as taking a daily pill – but I truly believe lifelong learning and self-development are key to gaining career and life confidence, so we all are better equipped for the challenges that will come our way.

Written By

Lynne Strong
Founder Action4Agriculture. Growing tomorrow's leaders today.

Opportunity
is calling you...
Remind me
in a year
Take it &
figure out

Opportunity Is Calling

A glance at this doodle might produce the response ***"Of course, I need to take the opportunity".*** Hitting the snooze button seems like the obvious "wrong choice". What do they say – "You snooze, you lose"?

Well... let's think this through.

Some people are going to hit the snooze button out of fear. Or comfort. Sometimes it helps to ask yourself, "If I don't take this opportunity, how will I feel about that in 5 years' time?" You might have heard of studies that show that the regrets people have are usually what they didn't do, rather than what they did.

One of our fears may be lack of confidence in our ability to succeed in the opportunity presented. We certainly do need to consider our resources. I have been impressed by the wisdom of a young man who turned down a big promotion, knowing he was not ready for it. It was not for lack of ambition or potential, but careful consideration and understanding of what he needed to succeed. Now, some years down the track, he is the General Manager of a 5-star hotel. His earlier decision has not held him back.

However, there are times where it is simply self-doubt. To identify if it is self-doubt or we are legitimately not ready, listening to others can help, especially those who work with us. If they are confident in our ability to do the job, and if the resources are in place to support us to do it, then perhaps we need to trust those things.

Another consideration is whether the opportunity is best for us. Sometimes opportunity comes knocking, perhaps in the form of headhunting. That's very flattering, but we have to consider whether this is really what we want to do.

Michelle Obama, in The Light We Carry, tells the story of Barack's choice to run for the presidency. He left the decision in her hands. Unless she was onboard, he would not run. That's a big call. Having a chance to run for President of the USA might seem like an opportunity too good to turn down. But he recognized a need to consider his relationships and how they would be impacted.

When weighing up an opportunity, you might take into account your values, your priorities, your goals. Look at the company culture, its vision, and mission. Is it something you can get excited about? Is the opportunity and timing right for me? There will be some uncertainties that I will navigate along the way if the opportunity is right for me. I don't have to have it all figured out.

If I say no, it might just be hitting the snooze button, and perhaps at another time, I will take the call.

- No need to say yes to every opportunity
- Don't make a decision out of a place of fear
- Consider your relationships, values, priorities, goals
- No now isn't no forever

When did you accept an opportunity without knowing how you will make it work? What did you learn from the experience?

Written By

Bernie McFarlane
Career Development Professional specialising in networking and job search. Connector of dots.

When did you not accept an opportunity? What did you learn from the experience?

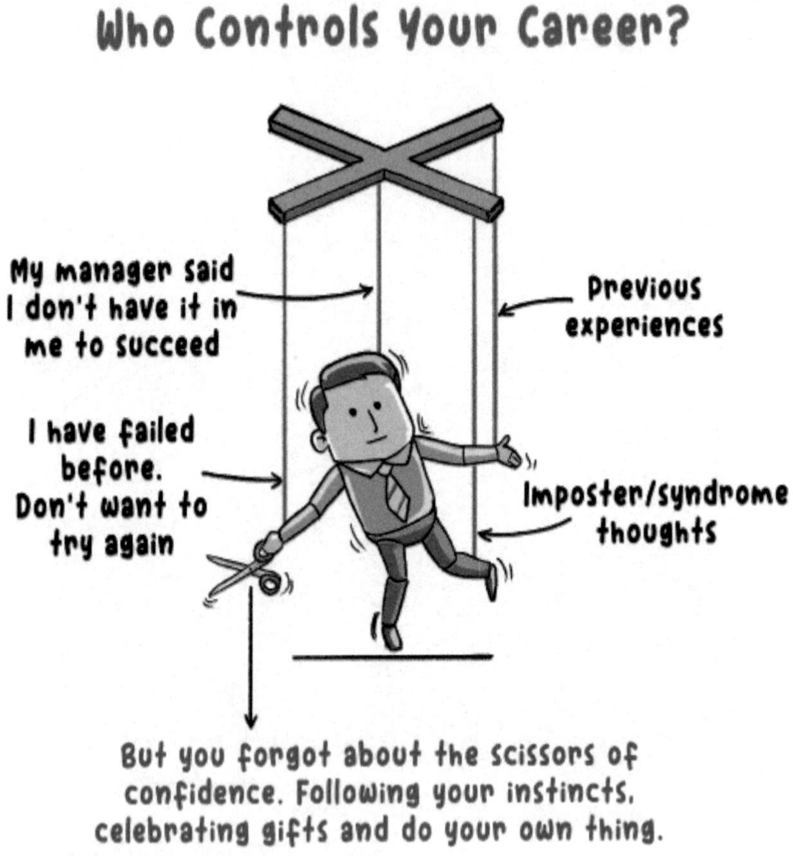
Who Controls Your Career?
My manager said I don't have it in me to succeed
Previous experiences
I have failed before. Don't want to try again
Imposter/syndrome thoughts
But you forgot about the scissors of confidence. Following your instincts, celebrating gifts and do your own thing.

Who Controls Your Career

Having moved from one country to another, this was one question that I keep dwelling on and eventually every time, I pick myself back up again and come back with some new ideas and reflections to work on with a NEW ME.
I am sure most of you can relate to me often, when your current employments don't go with the way that you anticipate and you are considering a career change or transition, you might end up with a similar question and end up with the plague of self-attacking thoughts of what went wrong with your last role ? Was it the way you responded or was it not staying close to the office gossip team that did not get you what you desired and deserved ???

Often, we evaluate ourselves and start to process inside our heads and accept that our perspective is flawed and biased and we attempt to validate this and in order to stay objective, we reach out for other's perspectives and are more open to hearing other opinions. But the key is going within and evaluating our own inner lens, and SELF Talk.

Inspired by the Louis Evans 5 Chairs 5 choices book, I highly recommend following your inner lens.

Image Credit: Louise Evans

THE 5 CHAIRS - Owner/Director/Creator @The5Chairs

Louis brings about an analogy of 5 different animals and coloured chairs to our behaviours and directs us to own our behaviours, master our communications as that shall determine our success.

When we sit one each of these, what attitudes and thoughts we develop Red chair, Chair described by Jackal, Yellow chair by Hedgehog, Green Chair of that of Meerkat, Blue Chair of Dolphin, Or Orange chair personified by Giraffe You always have a choice.

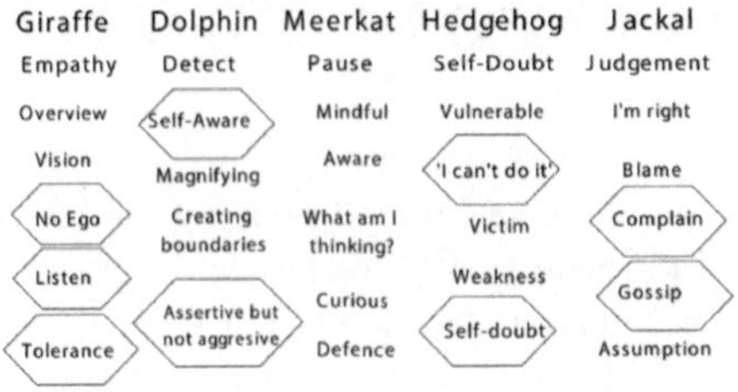

Option 1 : Get caught up in the whirlwind of thoughts, feelings of self-destructive thoughts of what did not go wrong and end up with "analysis paralysis" downward spiral

OR

Option 2 : Look at the entire aspect as a Learning Opportunity that helped you to learn about the attitudes of people, the perceptions that it created, the culture of the organisation and the people that influenced the situation, and your responses in the circumstance.

Steer your direction right by focusing on what works and what does not. One of the vital armours you need to hold on to, is your Confidence Campus

As this will help you to follow your own instincts, by celebrating gifts, and own your things.

Positive self-talk and Making a Conscious Choice of what you want to hold on to and how you get there will help you steer your path to success.

1. Be constructive with your goals and make an effort to make them exciting by adding on visualisations.
2. Make Action oriented plans focussing on the actions, rather than the end results.
3. Forgive yourself for some of the wrong moves if you had made earlier and take constructive decisions to not repeat them again. -

Written By

Shrivi Iyer
Collaborative Interdisciplinary Program Management Professional with over 30+ years of experience in International Human resources, Career Coaching and Talent Management.

Write your reflections on the doodle. Who or what controls your career?

What stops you in using the scissor?

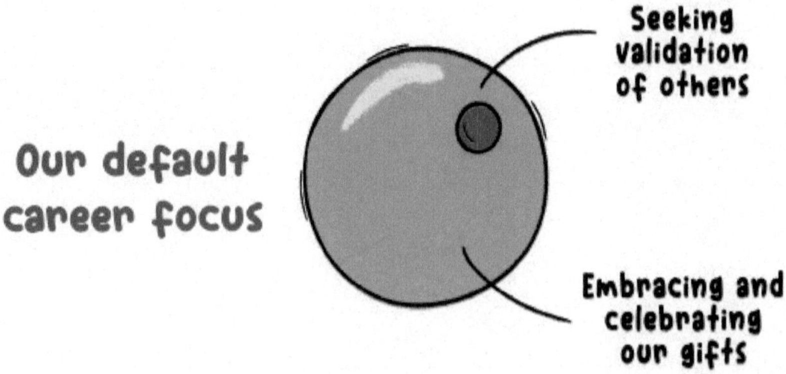
Our default career focus
Seeking validation of others
Embracing and celebrating our gifts

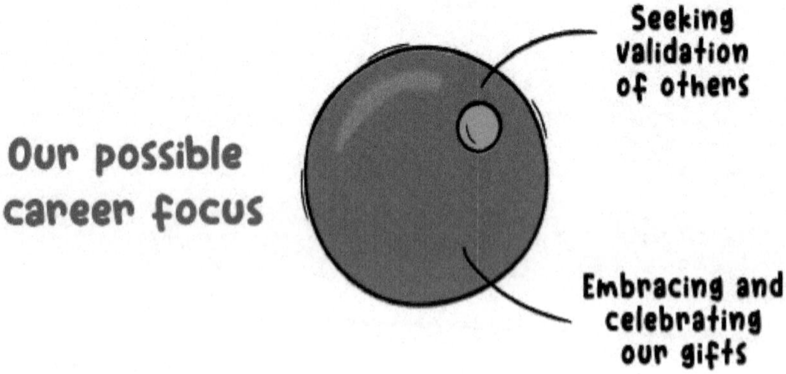
Our possible career focus
Seeking validation of others
Embracing and celebrating our gifts

Our Default Career Focus

The first thing that strikes me about this doodle is how alike the two visuals are – how easy it can be for the **default** mode to appear like the desired or **possible** mode! This makes me think about how when one is focused on seeking external validation, one might not even realise that it's what they are doing.

Embracing and celebrating our gifts starts with **self-awareness.** A clear understanding of what we are good at, what comes naturally to us, and how we create value and impact in our ecosystems. Taking self-assessments such as the Gallup StrengthsFinder, asking our colleagues, friends, and family about their experience of us, and taking time out regularly to introspect are impactful ways of building self-awareness.

Self-talk comes next. Self-talk is the most important conversation in our lives, yet very few pay attention to it. We are often kinder and more generous to, and more encouraging of others than ourselves. If we begin to speak to ourselves like we would to our best friend, for instance, we'd be so much more effective at embracing and celebrating our gifts.

Self-leadership is how we can become consistent and intentional about acknowledging and leveraging our gifts. Our own self is the most important person we'll ever lead. How we lead others is often a reflection of how we lead ourselves. Being rooted in our values, strengths, and gifts gives us the grit and resilience needed to stay relevant and impactful.

The smaller circle in the default mode "embracing and celebrating our gifts/ talents" also makes me think about how women tend to shrink because they are usually socially conditioned to take up less space. More often than not, and in most cultures, women are expected to blend in with the background and not be heard or seen as much. Due to years and years of this social programming, women tend to minimize their strengths and gifts, self-promote less, and seek out external validation to feel like they are indeed worth it. Systemic gender inequity across all sectors and age groups perpetuates this cycle of self-doubt among women.

The fact that this smaller circle is red makes me think of the human heart. Like how the heart is at the core of human life, so also is "embracing and celebrating our gifts/talents" at the core of our career success. Opening up our 'heart' expands our sense of what's possible. Expansion leads to clarity; clarity leads to conviction, and conviction leads to confidence. Confidence strengthens authenticity and creates space for self-compassion.

Just imagine what all we could accomplish if we just broke away from our **default** and stepped into **what's possible!**

What is your default career focus?

Written By

Meenakshi Iyer, MBA, ACC
I help Mid-career Technology Leaders, Women in Tech, and those who speak English as an additional language, be human-centered People and Change Leaders.

Is your career about seeking validation from others?

What stops you from celebrating your strengths and uniqueness?

Dig Your Calling

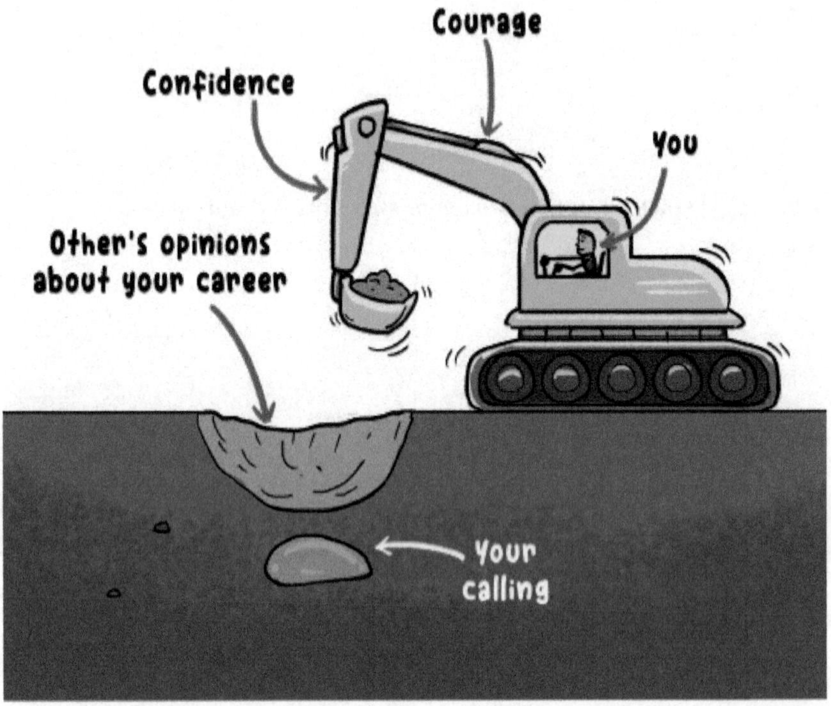

Dig Your Calling

To "dig your calling" means to discover and pursue your true purpose in life. It's about finding something that you're passionate about and that brings you fulfillment, and then working towards making it a reality.

It takes courage to follow your calling, but it's always worth it in the end. The support of loved ones and belief in oneself can make all the difference.

This doodle reminds me of the story of my favourite actor, Priyanka Chopra Jonas. Priyanka is a Bollywood actress who recognized her true calling to be a global entertainer, despite already achieving success in India. She faced many obstacles in pursuing a career in Hollywood, including doubts about her acting abilities and cultural differences. However, with her determination, confidence, and resilience, Priyanka captured the attention of Hollywood with her lead role in a hit drama, eventually appearing in major films. Her story reminds me that pursuing our calling requires perseverance, resilience, and confidence in our abilities. Her accomplishments illustrate how courage and self-confidence can help us redefine our career trajectories and achieve success beyond our wildest dreams.

Often, others may have opinions about our career choices or calling that may not align with our own desires or aspirations. However, it's important to have confidence in ourselves and what we want, even in the face of criticism or doubt. It can take courage to pursue our calling, as it may involve stepping outside of our comfort zones or taking risks.

Ultimately, it's up to us to dig deep within ourselves and identify what truly brings us happiness and fulfillment. This may require self-reflection, exploring different career paths or hobbies, and taking action towards making our dreams a reality.

By following our calling, we can find a sense of purpose and live a more fulfilling life. It may not always be an easy path, but the journey towards our goals can be just as rewarding as achieving them.

Written By

Gauri Gokhale
Trusted Talent Partner | Candidate Coach | Talent Strategy Advisor

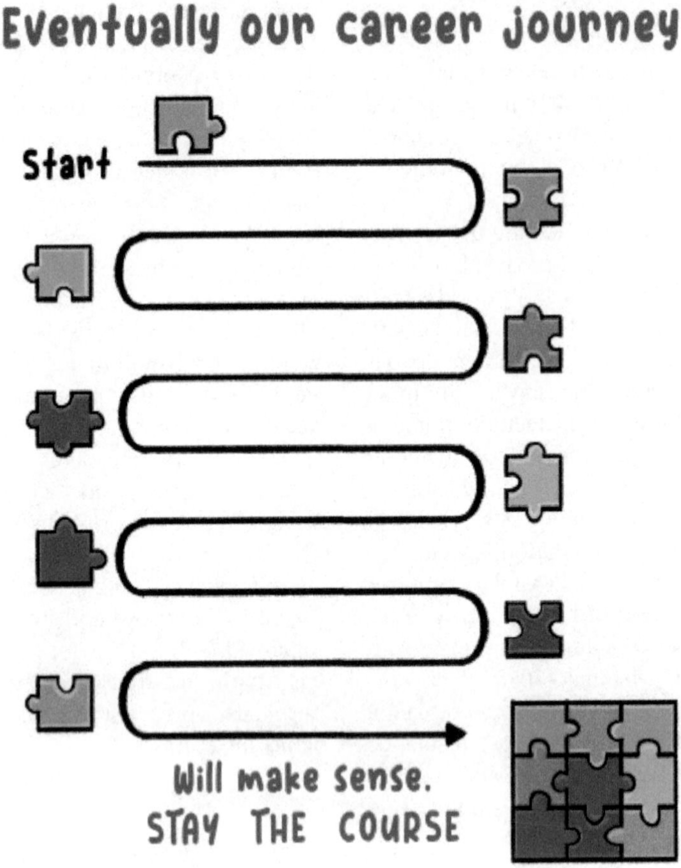
Eventually our career journey
Start
Will make sense.
STAY THE COURSE

Your Career Story Will Eventually Make Sense

One of my favourite sayings is ***"different is better than better."*** When it comes to putting yourself forward as the right person for a task, being different is better than being better.

Each person is unique. You have something to offer that nobody else in the world does. Identify what that is and be proud of it. Your uniqueness comes from your personality, life experience, values, and wisdom.

It includes the cumulative effect of all the jobs you have had, including volunteer work. When changing careers, some people think their past career is a hindrance to being considered for a new job or industry. It's as if we have been labelled one thing and can never be another. Rather, coming from a completely different discipline can give us a perspective that others might not have. It enriches, rather than detracts from, what we bring to our new role.

A client was working with me to help him break into the radio industry. In one conversation, he told me, ***"My previous job working in a bar is the one where I learned the most about dealing with people."*** Then there's the journalist who reinvented herself as a chef. She transferred her sense of curiosity from reporting to exploring new ideas on the plate. And that's the key - it's the transferability of skills from one profession to the next - identifying them, highlighting them (your "different"), and applying them.

Nothing is wasted. Every job you have ever had, you can learn something from. Even if you had the misfortune to be in an undesirable situation. If nothing else, you learn what not to do again or what to avoid; you may have learned something about yourself and your resilience and perhaps gained more compassion and empathy for others' difficult situations.

Reflection is a key part of this. As John Dewey said, ***"We do not learn from experience...we learn from reflecting on experience."*** If you look back over your career so far, you can discover that each experience has taught you something. Be proud of all the jobs you have had - from the humblest to the highest achievements.

Some of the pieces of this puzzle might be the people you meet, the connections you collect along the way. These are just as priceless as the skills and experience you gain from each step in your career.

Look after your connections. There's a lot of truth in the saying, ***"If you want to go fast, go alone, if you want to go far, go together."*** When you nurture the relationships along the way, the opportunities that appear are often better than you could even have dreamed of for yourself.

Nothing is wasted if you know how to connect the dots. And remember that jigsaws require patience.

To summarize:

- Each step in our career builds on the previous.
- Reflection is key.
- Each person we meet along the way plays a role.
- Nothing is wasted.

Write your reflections on the doodle.

Written By

Bernie McFarlane
Career Development Professional specialising in networking and job search. Connector of dots.-

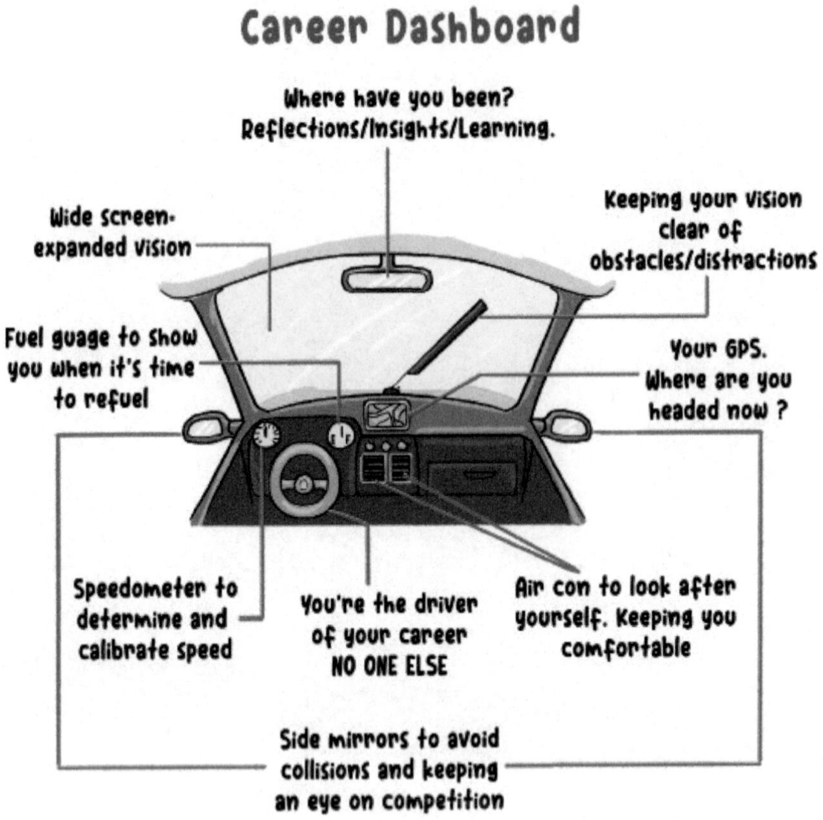
Career Dashboard
Where have you been? Reflections/Insights/Learning.
Wide screen- expanded vision
Keeping your vision clear of obstacles/distractions
Fuel guage to show you when it's time to refuel
Your GPS. Where are you headed now ?
Speedometer to determine and calibrate speed
You're the driver of your career NO ONE ELSE
Air con to look after yourself. Keeping you comfortable
Side mirrors to avoid collisions and keeping an eye on competition

Career Dashboard

My dad had a long career, over 40+ years in the same organisation. He started there young and with much to learn. I feel his dashboard would have had a very wide and open screen. Back when my dad started work, I'm not sure he knew of or there was much of a career dashboard. He went to work, did his job, and did it with much dedication, and he progressed through the ranks as his skills and experience grew. There was much simplicity to his career back then, no need for a dashboard, just get in and drive!

My own career has been different. This doodle provides some insight into those differences.

Wide screen - representing the need for vision, and as my career has changed and grown, my need for clarity has grown. The need to look around and take notice of what is happening around me, finding gratitude in what I have seen, heard, and done, and to use this awareness to continue to make decisions based on what I need or want in my life.

Where have you been? - Reflecting and learning have been important areas across my career to date. Where have I come from? What have I learned along the way? These insights are constant, always something to consider as I make decisions for what's happening now and tomorrow.

Windscreen wipers - These have provided that sense of comfort in knowing that they are there to clear my vision. These are represented by my strengths, my connections, my skills and experience, and my confidence - sometimes I just need to remember that they are there and can be actioned by me, no need to rely on anyone else.

Your GPS - I like a road map, I like to know where I am heading, there is much confidence and trust that comes from my GPS, and often this is created from the screen and reflections that are always before me. And even if my GPS isn't working, although it may cause some uneasiness, I always know my windscreen wipers are there to clear the way in the moment.

Look after self - With a click of a switch, the air con is on, and it's comforting to know that what I need to look after me is always within arm's reach. Sometimes I click on the heater because I know what I need, why I need it, and when I need it.
Fuel gauge - Such an empowering visual to see how I am tracking. I don't need to rely on someone else to tell me, to give me feedback, to acknowledge my efforts. I can provide all of that to myself with just a glance at the gauge.

Side mirrors - I definitely feel like in my dad's career, there was no need for these. There was no competition or chance of collision because there were far fewer people on the career journey. People back then stayed in their lane; they didn't know about other lanes, let alone other roads or destinations. Whereas now, with all the access we have to people's lives, we can make the comparison, we can see what other journeys people are taking, and we might choose to go on those roads too. That's why we need these side mirrors.

Speedometer - My career speed has been up and down, and this speed has matched my life speed. Once again, it has been under my control, which I am extremely grateful for. I truly don't like tailgaters pushing me along, getting me to go faster than I need or want.

Steering wheel - I love having the control of my steering wheel. It has allowed me to experience my career in the way that I needed or wanted. It's not to say I haven't taken recommendations from others to try another destination because I certainly have, but with the control in my hands, it means the benefits and challenges along the way have been for me to learn and grow from. I have found that has been the important element to keep driving my career, one that I love and am proud of.
Your career dashboard may look or sound similar to mine, or it may look and sound completely different - and that's exactly as it should be. There are many different makes and models of cars and careers on offer. Choose the one that you like now, the one that provides the comfort or confidence that you need now, knowing that you can update in the future if you need.

As for my Dad, he may not have had a career dashboard, but he had a career that he was proud of. The lesson for me is that sometimes we don't need all the bells and whistles to do what we need in life. We just need to choose to live the life we have.

Love you, Dad. xo.

Written By

Sharon Kilmartin
Leadership Coach, Group Facilitator and 'The Great Recharge' facilitator
Supporting individuals to be the best they can be!

Write your reflections on the doodle.

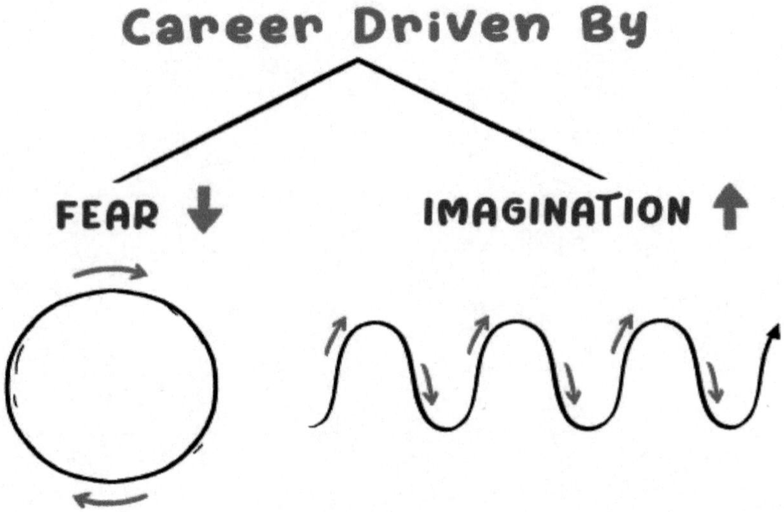
Career Driven By
FEAR
IMAGINATION

Career Driven by Fear and Imagination

Hey there, my career-savvy friends! It's time to talk about a topic that could be the difference between living your best work life or being trapped in a soul-sucking job. Today, we're talking about the difference between a career driven by fear versus one driven by imagination.

First things first, let's talk about the fear-driven career. You know the type. They're always worried about making mistakes, they double and triple-check everything, and they're constantly looking over their shoulders to make sure they're not going to get fired. These people are living in a constant state of anxiety, and it's not doing them any favors.

Fear-driven careers limit your potential. You're not going to take risks, try new things, or push boundaries if you're too afraid of failure. You'll miss out on opportunities to grow and learn, and you'll never be able to truly express your creativity. Plus, all that fear and anxiety can lead to burnout, which is no bueno.

Now let's talk about the imagination-driven career. These people are always thinking outside the box, dreaming up new ideas, and taking calculated risks. They're not afraid to fail, because they know that failure is just a stepping stone to success. They're constantly growing, learning, and pushing themselves to be better.

Imagination-driven careers are the ones that really take off. You're not just doing the bare minimum to get by, you're creating something truly unique and special. You're bringing your own flavor to the table, and people are going to notice. You're not just another cog in the machine, you're a game-changer.

So how do you shift from a fear-driven career to an imagination-driven one? Well, it's not going to happen overnight, but there are a few things you can do to get started.

First, start taking risks. You don't have to go bungee jumping or skydiving (unless you want to, of course), but start small. Try a new restaurant, take a different route to work, or talk to someone new. The more comfortable you get with taking risks, the more confident you'll become.

Next, embrace failure. It's going to happen, so you might as well make friends with it. Learn from your mistakes and use them as stepping stones to success. The more you fail, the more you'll grow and learn.

Finally, start flexing those creative muscles. You don't have to be an artist or a writer to be creative. Start brainstorming ideas for your projects, think about new ways to approach problems, and challenge yourself to think outside the box.

Remember, your career is your own personal journey. You can either let fear hold you back or let your imagination take you to new heights. So what are you waiting for? Let's get creative and start living our best work lives!

Credits: Originated with CHATGPT AI, polished by Naishadh Gadani

CHATGTP is property of OpenAI

Here are some questions you can ask yourself to determine whether your career is driven by fear or imagination:

1. What motivates me to pursue my career? Is it a sense of purpose, creativity, and inspiration,
2. Am I truly passionate about my work, or am I just going through the motions because it feels
3. Have I taken risks and pursued opportunities that align with my passions and interests, or
4. Do I feel fulfilled and inspired by my work, or do I feel like something is missing and I am not
5. Am I making decisions based on what I truly want, or am I being influenced by the opinions
6. Do I feel a sense of purpose and meaning in my work, or do I feel like my job is just a means to an end?

Written By

Naishadh Gadani
Engineer turned Career Practitioner. Author. Doodler. Presenter. Non-TEDx Speaker. Helping people design their careers.

Showing-off
on social media
Doing
amazing
things
Doing the
same amazing
things you do
Your
career
Other
people's
career

Social Media and Your Career

A garnish is intended to complement and enhance the main ingredient in the drink to which it is added. An olive or a fruit twist adds ornamental appeal to a cocktail, might even imbue a whisper of flavour, and be a potentially edible treat after the drink is finished. Modern garnishes are much more flamboyant than the traditional trimmings. Today's bartenders want to create maximum visual appeal. To construct, then photograph a work of art. To generate a social media sensation.

Social media is a powerful career tool for everyone, not just bartenders. Potential employers routinely research job applicants, examining online activity and profiles before offering interviews or appointments. In our contemporary world of work, where employment opportunities are rapidly and continuously evolving, online engagement provides invaluable access to learning and work openings.

Alongside the tools of any trade sit the skills we need to find and carry out work within our chosen profession. To find and secure work, we need to research opportunities, identify knowledge and skill gaps, set goals, communicate our strengths and achievements, and network. As one of many career tools, professionally focussed social media platforms can be especially useful in each of these areas. Worth, quality, and integrity can, however, be difficult to gauge on social media platforms. To quote Racheed Ogunlaru, "All the tools, techniques and technology in the world are nothing without the head, heart and hands to use them wisely, kindly and mindfully".

What we need, then, is a recipe for constructive, professional engagement with social media. A recipe that each of us adapts according to the ingredients we have on hand.

Basic Recipe for a Social Media Garnish

Ingredients:

- Willingness to learn
- Time to read and think before writing
- A known purpose
- Focus
- Work we care about
- Integrity

Method:

- Explore the social media platforms most closely aligned with my career direction, goals, and aspirations. Identify the features of each platform and the type of information that is being posted. Decide which platform/s I am most comfortable with and reflect on why I feel this way.

- Read and consider posts from people I admire. Learn from their writing. Follow or connect with people and organisations whose writings, career directions, and actions are inspiring to me.
- Before posting, consider my purpose.
- Note to self: online activity builds my public profile. My posts, conversations, and engagements over time will demonstrate my interests, values, achievements, and integrity.

Most importantly ....

Keep doing the amazing work I do, regardless of social media. Remind myself, a garnish, no matter how spectacular, is not the main ingredient. It is the taste test; the long, cool, drink; that counts.

Cheers!

How has what you see and perceive on social media impacted your career and your perception of success? Write your reflection

Written By

Leigh Pickstone
Career Development Practitioner, Facilitator, and Teacher Empowering people to successfully navigate their career journey.

Personal Branding Paradox
How people should build a brand
How people build a brand
Posting on social media
Communication strategy
Who do you serve?
Who's your audience?
What's your unique perspective?
Determining the problem you solve
Identifying your strengths and values
Taking stock of how people perceive you
What's your why?
Taking a deep dive into your work

Personal Branding Paradox

Personal brand value is linked to reputation and trust.

While we cannot control the communication or perception of our personal brand 100% of the time, we can certainly develop and take responsibility for the foundations of creating an authentic personal brand. Creating strong foundations of knowledge and behaving in a way that aligns with our 'why', strengths, and values can maintain an authentic and resilient personal brand that will weather change and aspects of life outside of our control.

A strong personal brand is about having an insurance policy to protect our reputation and professional value. When we voice our opinion on social media, if we have an authentic and consistent personal brand, it will more likely result in us being perceived with trust and respect, even if the audience doesn't always agree with our views. There are numerous examples of celebrities (sporting and political), with a strong personal brand, saying and doing things considered inappropriate or illegal, who are saved from long-term negative impact on their careers because of having a recognizable and trusted personal brand. An 'ordinary' person's career is less likely to survive.

The more developed the personal branding foundation, the more stable and recognizable the message will be. Without this, any written and verbal communication on social media will be inconsistent, and the lack of alignment with purpose will limit the audience. It may seem counter-intuitive, but the more you "know yourself" and communicate consistently, the more you will develop trust and respect with a wider audience. This will always be an asset for your career and life.

Written By

Nicola Barnard
Over 10 years of Career Development Consulting, assisting adults across a wide range of roles and industries to communicate their value.

Be Yourself

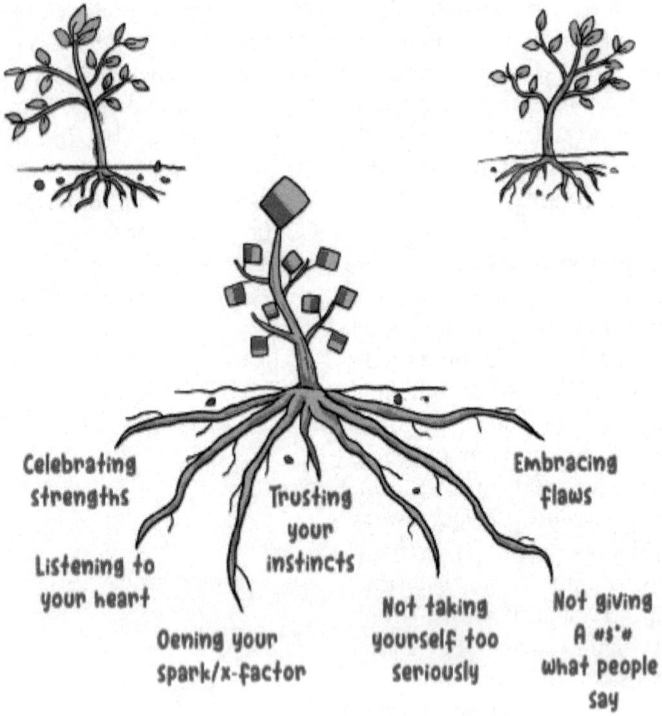
Celebrating strengths
Trusting your instincts
Embracing flaws
Listening to your heart
Oening your spark/x-factor
Not taking yourself too seriously
Not giving A #$*# what people say

Be Yourself

Last week, I observed my 2-year-old niece as she encountered a new experience. Her parents decided to move out from the house that she was born in, the only home she had ever known until now. As the movers and packers started going about their job, she watched them quietly. She knew something big was happening; all her toys were being packed up, the furniture was being dismantled, and bags and cartons were being carried out of the house by strange, muscly, tattooed men.

A usually feisty little girl, she hid her personality behind a veil and watched the men with keen eyes, while holding on to her mum. A little scared but also a little curious.

Then, one of them flashed her a smile. She didn't smile back, although you could see that she wanted to. After a few minutes, he waved at her and said hi. She loosened up and felt a bit special. Her eyes lit up, and she smiled back. As more time passed, she became comfortable with them being around. Slowly but surely, she inched closer to the men. As one of them sat down on the floor to dismantle her toy chest, she walked up to him and started communicating with gestures. After a few more minutes, she gathered her courage and touched the tattoo on his arm and said, "What this?" in her broken and limited vocabulary. He smiled back and said, "Tattoo." She repeated after him, "Tato." He laughed a little, and she laughed with him.

So much of what you see in this doodle was on display. At first, she observed, but with time she couldn't help but be herself. She trusted her instincts about the men, she listened to her heart, and stayed true to her curiosity about them. She owned her x-factor, embraced her flaws and her broken vocabulary, and made the first contact to communicate with complete strangers.

Children have an effortless way of being themselves. It's because they don't know how to be anything else. However, as we grow older, we get conditioned by so many different things. Societal norms, expectations from friends and family, job roles – all this influences us, and even encourages us, to adopt a homogenous personality, one that is constantly trying to fit in with the rest of the world.

But we forget that we were never built to fit in. We were built to be our unique selves. So, if lately you're not feeling much like yourself, all you need to do is look at your roots, go back to the inner child within you, and adopt behaviours that make you uniquely you!

Write your reflections on the doodle.

Written By

Sangeeta Mulchandani

Sangeeta Mulchandani is an author, speaker, and startup coach focused on empowering 1 million entrepreneurs globally.

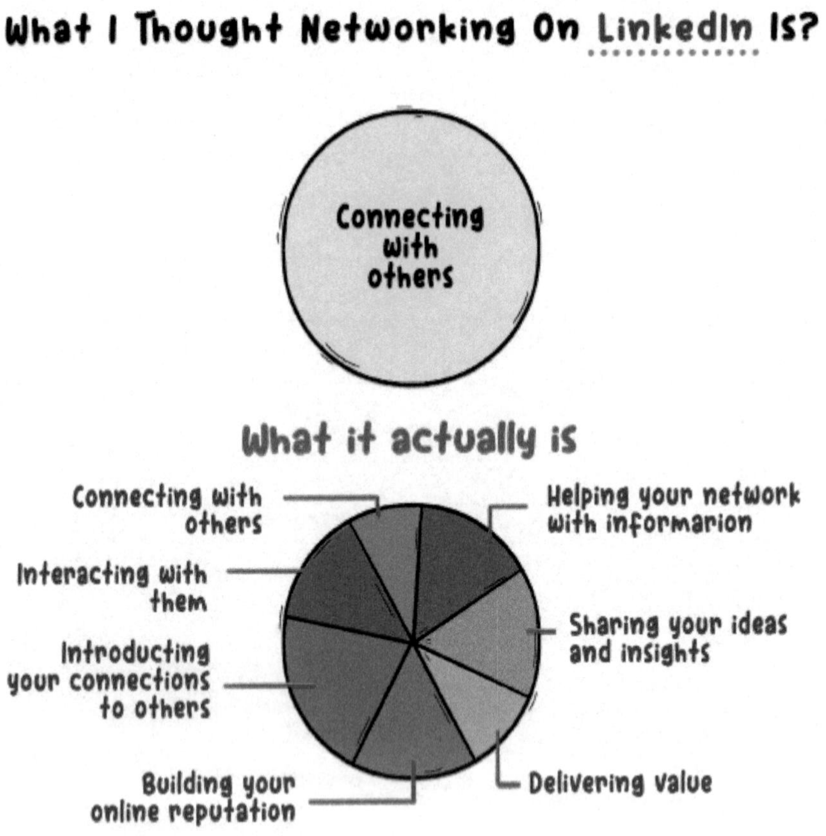
What I Thought Networking On LinkedIn Is?
Connecting with others
What it actually is
Connecting with others
Interacting with them
Introducting your connections to others
Building your online reputation
Helping your network with informarion
Sharing your ideas and insights
Delivering value

What I Thought Networking on LinkedIn Is?

LinkedIn is possibly the most underused business networking tool in the world!

Many people see this as just another social media tool for connecting with others - they rarely see the true value of what lies underneath.

LinkedIn is a plethora of resources for everyone working or looking to access the world of work. Businesses advertise, and you can access free training, CPD and connect with others who are in similar sectors to yourself. You are able to build and develop your own online personal brand, creating a live and interactive CV with far more than a CV could ever showcase
.

It's also great for peer-to-peer learning and you can join groups of interest such as professional bodies or other local businesses. For me, it's a great place to share ideas and keep up to date on industry and legislative changes, a one-stop shop with everything you need. The online training is really comprehensive, with many courses being free.

Recruiters are constantly searching for candidates on LinkedIn and I have personally been approached - imagine others approaching you for work as your personal brand, photo (ensure it's professional!), qualifications, and experience are inspiring others to reach out.

When jobs are advertised, they are shared by others in the business who reach out to offer informal chats. It's a great way of figuring out if a business is a right fit for you and your skills. This is the start of building up a picture of what an organisation or sector is like and how they portray themselves and the opportunities available.

Every time I sign in, there is an abundance of useful articles, fellow connections sharing resources, and some connections moving on to new job opportunities - it's the most efficient way of interacting with others in your sector or the sector you are looking to break into.

I thought this was a boring social media tool purely for businessmen, but how wrong I was! The more you put in - the more you are rewarded - LinkedIn has enriched my working life in a way no words can describe.

Be careful - it can become rather addictive, but in a positive way for your career and personal development.

Get signed up, get following, and connect - your networking journey starts here.

Written By

Sally-Ann Monger
Careers Adviser | Registered Career Development Professional | Career Development Institute Member | BACVW Certified CV Writer | Supporting Neurodiversity & SEND

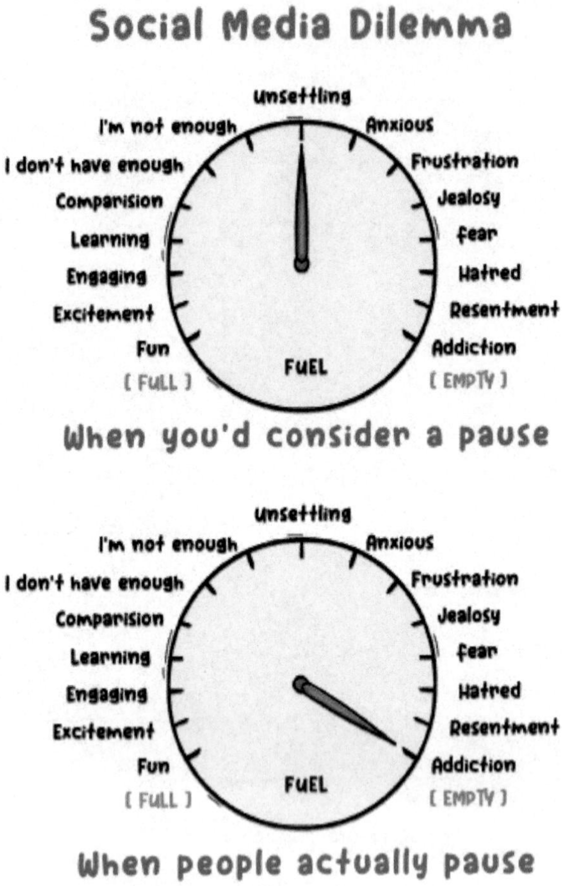
Social Media Dilemma
Unsettling
I'm not enough
Anxious
I don't have enough
Frustration
Comparision
Jealosy
Learning
fear
Engaging
Hatred
Excitement
Resentment
Fun
Addiction
[FULL]
FUEL
[EMPTY]
When you'd consider a pause
Unsettling
I'm not enough
Anxious
I don't have enough
Frustration
Comparision
Jealosy
Learning
fear
Engaging
Hatred
Excitement
Resentment
Fun
Addiction
[FULL]
FUEL
[EMPTY]
When people actually pause

Social Media Dilemma

The constant scroll, the endless feed, A never-ending cycle, hard to break free.

Before it's too late, press pause, Disconnect, and find your own cause.

Take a step back, and breathe in the present, Find peace in the now and let go of resent.

Before it's too late, reclaim your time, Disconnect from the screens and let your mind shine.

Don't let social media consume you whole, Find balance in your day and make your own goals.

Press pause, because it's time to choose your fate, And live your life, before it's too late.

Credits: Originated with CHATGPT AI, polished by Sangeeta Mulchandani

Written By

Sangeeta Mulchandani
Sangeeta is an author, speaker, and startup coach focused on empowering 1 million entrepreneurs globally.

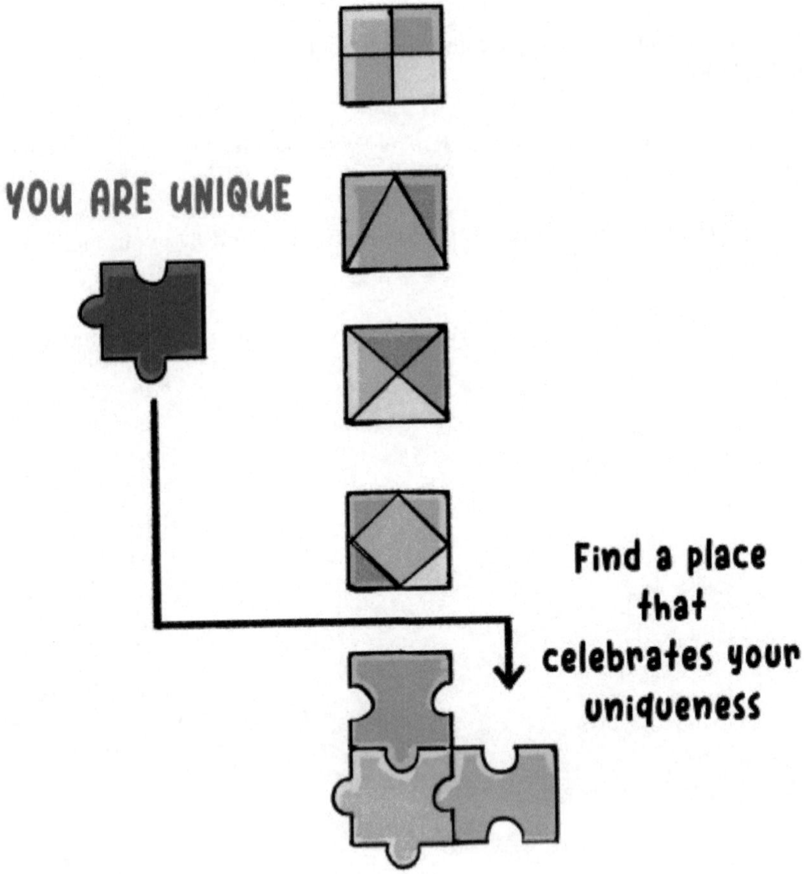
YOU ARE UNIQUE
Find a place that celebrates your uniqueness

You're Unique. Find a Place That Celebrates It.

Have you ever been in a workplace, situation, or with a group of people where you felt out of place without really knowing why? It might make you feel like you are marching to the beat of your own drum, while others are waltzing to another tune. Or feeling that you are one part of a missing jigsaw puzzle, trying Tetris-like to fit in and not quite aligning with the other pieces. I know I have felt that way on more than one occasion, perhaps you have too?

Sometimes we need to take 'survival' jobs. I have found myself in that situation at different times, taking the first thing I could find without researching the role. Other times, I've taken roles without finding out about the work culture or career growth opportunities, for example. Over time, I felt myself becoming stifled, trapped, and losing my sense of self and confidence. This was particularly true when I worked in toxic work culture environments.

What can we do to help find our tribe? My biggest tip would be to give yourself permission to take time to reflect and explore some of the strategies listed below:

- Spend time getting to know yourself through self-reflection activities to gain self-clarity on who you are and what you believe in (i.e., your interests, strengths, skills, personality, values, education/lifelong learning, and where it is going to take you).
- Identify and align your core values.
- Identify your workplace attractors and which ones would be non-negotiables. Are they security, location, work environment aesthetics, relationships, recognition, contribution, work fit, flexibility, learning, responsibility, feeling of acceptance, innovation, or something else?
- Research company cultures. Take the time to research the company's values, beliefs, and culture to see if they align with your own. Look for diversity and inclusion initiatives the company actively takes, such as ERGs (Employee Resource Groups) or training around biases and cultural differences.
- Read job descriptions carefully. Look at the job descriptions and see if they mention anything about valuing diversity, uniqueness, and individuality. This is generally an indication that the company values diversity and unique perspectives.

- Connect with people. Connect with current or past employees, either through LinkedIn, Glassdoor, or networking events, and ask them about their experience working for the company. This can give you a sense if the company is inclusive and values unique perspectives or not.
- Be yourself during interviews (while maintaining an appropriate level of professionalism). Be yourself during job interviews and let your unique perspective and personality shine through. Companies that value unique perspectives and diversity will appreciate this and respond positively.
- Attend events and job fairs. Attend job fairs and events targeting diverse talent, such as those hosted by organisations aimed at a specific culture or diversity in general. These events might be a great place to find a company culture that aligns with your individuality.

Remember that finding a workplace that truly values your uniqueness may take time and effort, but ultimately it will lead to a fulfilling and satisfying career.

Write your reflections on the doodle.

Written By

Jennifer (Jenn) Barfield RPCDP, PCDAA, CHATP
Career Development Professional.
Empowering people to sustain action-oriented hope. Specialises in Veteran and Military Spouse career journeys.

Ways to Destroy Your Reputation
Time it takes to build a reputation
A single tweet or social media post to destroy it.

The Conscious Social Media User

It was in 2019 that I decided to shut down all of my social media accounts. Facebook, deactivated. LinkedIn, closed. Snapchat, deleted. My actions were a response to the toxicity that I had found myself in socially and personally and were also informed by the writings, experience, and thoughts of Cal Newport. His book that I was listening to at the time, "Deep Work: Rules for Focused Success in a Distracted World", spurred me into taking this, what may be considered by some, extreme action.

Fast forward to 2023 and I am now a conscious user of one social media platform, LinkedIn. A 'conscious user' by my definition involves connecting with people and organisations for the purpose of remaining engaged in matters and industry that are relevant to my areas of professional and amateur interest. There is no absent-minded scrolling where hours tick by or use during times where I should be working or embracing boredom. So far, it appears to be paying off! For example, the opportunity to write this article came from connecting with Naishadh on LinkedIn.

Just as my use of social media has evolved, so too has the speed and power of social media influence. There are several positive cases where social media has been leveraged for its speed and power of influence:

- **Twitter:** WeRateDogs (@dog_rates) in partnership with 15/10 Foundation (@15outof10) to make shelter dogs with medical needs more adoptable.
- **Facebook:** After a six-year-old girl's Aunty posted on Facebook asking for people to help make her niece's birthday special during a COVID-19 lockdown, over 180 cards and 15 packages were sent in response (Dickson, 2020).
- **TikTok:** Numerous business success stories describing increased content views, engagement, ad recall, return on advertising spend and conversion rates (TikTok, 2022).

Sliding toward the other end of the scale, people have lost jobs, been demoted, and have all but decimated their reputation in organisations, industries and the public eye after uploading a tweet, post or video. Even in jest, the reputation of a person or organisation that has taken years to build can be toppled by a single poorly thought-out tweet or social media post (Eniola, 2020). Therefore, I suggest that a conscious user should also be a conscious uploader. To achieve this, I believe one needs to ask before they upload, **would I be comfortable with this being on the cover of every news outlet around the world? If not, do not post.**

With the emerging engagement I am now experiencing with LinkedIn and through reflecting on my absence from social media, I can see that, to borrow from social worker and founder of Distinction Co. Patricia Mura Desert (2021), it is not that I want to be away from it all, but rather, I need my social media platforms to be positively impactful.

References

Desert, P. M. (2021). Social Consciousness in the Digital Age: Using Social Media To Create A Better World. The New Social Worker: The Social Work Careers Magazine.

Dickson, C. (2020). B.C. girl celebrates 6th birthday with letters from around the world. CBC. https://www.cbc.ca/news/canada/british-columbia/charlie-manning-6th-birthday-1.5685969

Eniola, A. (2020). How a Single Tweet Can Destroy or Build your Brand Reputation. Jeff Bullas: Win at Business and Life in a Digital World. https://www.jeffbullas.com/twitter-brand-reputation/

Newport, C. (2016). Deep work: rules for focused success in a distracted world. Piatkus.

TikTok. (2022). Success Stories About TikTok Advertising | TikTok for Business. TikTok for Business. https://www.tiktok.com/business/en-AU/inspiration

Written By

Sarah Marie Fogarty
PhD Candidate @ Edith Cowan University
I apply multidisciplinary experience, creative systems thinking and research skills to navigate challenges in the education sector.

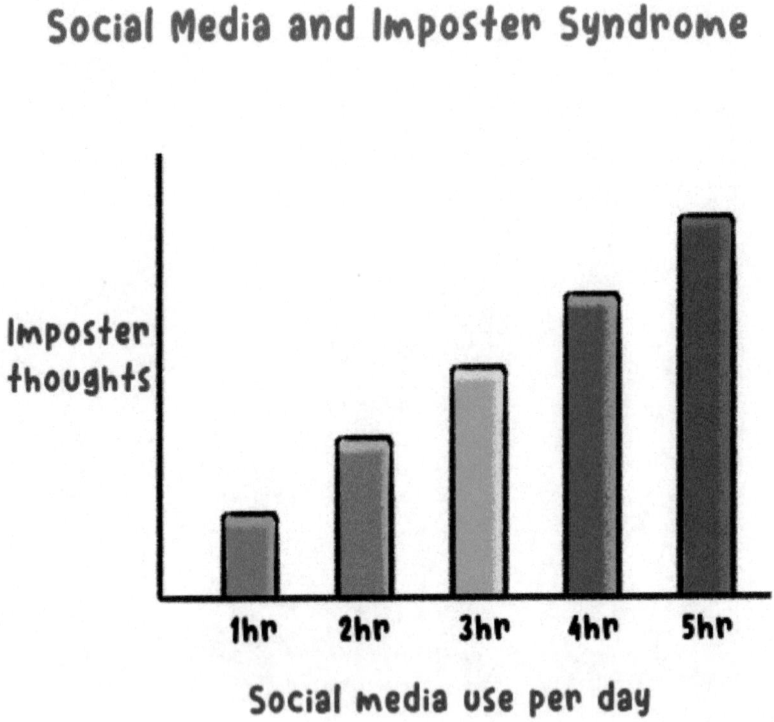
Social Media and Imposter Syndrome
Imposter thoughts
1hr
2hr
3hr
4hr
5hr
Social media use per day

Social Media and Imposter Syndrome

I was randomly surfing Facebook while at work, and a post caught my attention enough to raise my eyebrows. It was my mom who had a status update check-in at a cemetery nearby. Cemetery? Why would she check-in into a cemetery? As I got home, it all made sense to me. Mom was on her first international holiday visiting us, and she was learning how to use the check-in function on Facebook so she could feed her location updates to her friends in India, and they could see all the places she was visiting. I found it funny that she chose to check-in at this nearby cemetery of all places, but that was the location that popped up. Interestingly, the internet and social media have made older generations tech-savvy and adapt to new technology way faster than anything.

With the increase in internet access, smart devices, cheaper data, and increasing platforms, social media now plays a significant impact on our lives. It has given the power in the hands of millions to see the world, have a window into our personal worlds, connect with people, and voice their opinions.

Economics and psychology are now studied differently, given the power that social media has given to individuals. The value of social currency like 'number of likes' and 'number of followers' is as valuable as real money.

It's the sizzle more than the sausage that matters on social media. We are all hungry for attention, which on social media is 'Likes', 'Comments', 'Thumbs up', 'Views', 'Followers'. To seek this social currency, we choose to write the perfect content, post perfect pictures, choose the correct time. Social media posts have evolved into a whole new subject on its own.

Self-image and social consciousness take priority in the way we do and see things. Unlike in the past, the power to control the media was largely in the hands of a few newspapers, and television news.

Today, it is in the hands of millions. Reality is exposed way faster than before. The marketplace has a whole new dimension. Social media has opened up a new world of opportunities for small businesses, creating a new stream of wealth creation.

We spend a lot more time on social media and complain about being busy and not having enough time in the day. Given the technological evolution, social media will keep evolving, and so will we. It is now a part of who we are!

Written By

Dipti Pandit
Growth Leader and Customer Champion
Board Member at Australia Professionals of Colour at Australia Passionate about helping young professionals to transition and succeed in leadership roles.

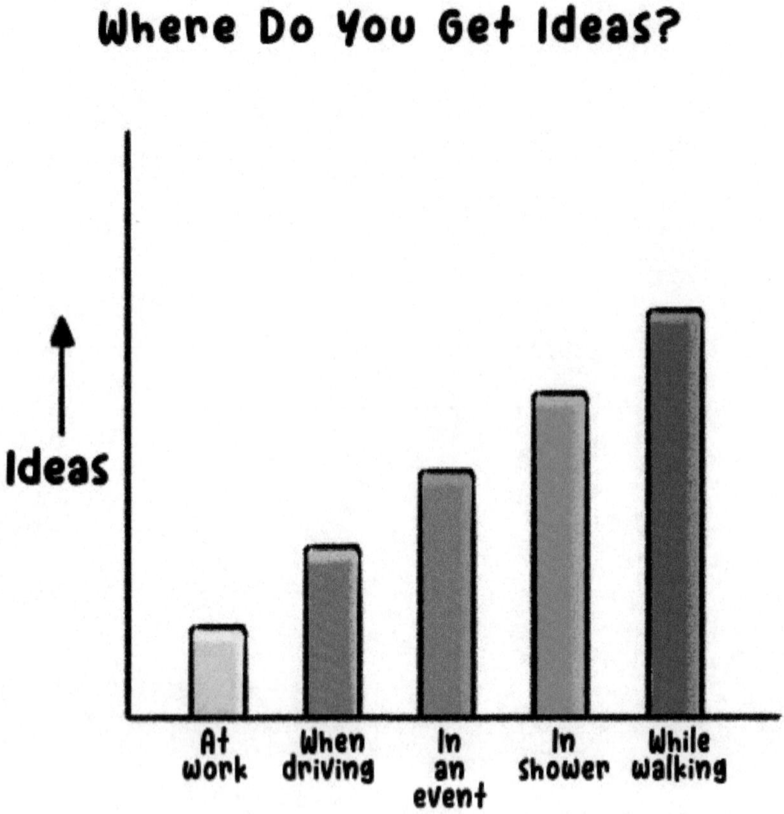
Where Do You Get Ideas?
Ideas
At work
When driving
In an event
In Shower
While walking

Where Do You Get Ideas?

It was Covid that brought these thoughts to my head: thoughts of despair, wondering when it would end, and how I would cope. I was selling dental practices, both large and small, with the larger ones being snapped up by health funds and amalgamators, which brought impressive broker fees my way.

Then it hit. The pandemic. People are suffering everywhere and dental practices are closed - forever, according to the news. It was very difficult to sell a business that had $0 turnover and no sign of ever opening again.

So, I sat at my desk, thinking it was the best place to come up with ideas. Unfortunately, it was not. The stress just by being in an office wasn't conducive to any positive thoughts, let alone coming to a CBD that looked like the apocalypse had hit. I had a dubious permit to work that enabled me to come into the ghost town that used to be heralded as the most liveable city in the world.

This doodle represents to me where my ideas do come from. Not at work, not at events, or even when trying to write. Nothing is worse than having all these ideas rattling around in your head, and then, when a blank piece of paper is put in front of you, it's like your mind has been erased of all those thoughts and you can no longer string a meaningful sentence together, let alone some life-changing ideas.

The shower? Yes, a great place to switch off and get clean. But walking? Oh, the walking. Five kilometres and no longer than two hours at a time (later reduced to one hour). No traffic, not many people around, and those who were around crossed the road if you looked like you were going to get too close. And do not dare to cough!

But that's where the ideas came. No music, just the sounds around me, of which there were not many. The wind, birds singing, the perfect time to clear my thoughts and bring back positive vibes for the job search ahead.

Fifteen years of working for myself - who would want to employ a middle-aged white guy whose privileges had long since departed?

If nothing else, the pandemic brought me a certain inner peace, a slightly slower pace, and an ability to detach myself from the game of life, take stock, take a breath, and enter again when ready. It also provided me with a new job, in a new industry, and renewed joy in work.

Write your reflections on the doodle.

Written By

Alex Barritt
Business Development Manager & Relationship Builder. Still living in Melbourne, following a 2 week holiday from the UK in November 2000.

NO MATTER THE SIZE OF
YOUR STEPS
BE
PROUD OF
YOUR
PROGRESS

Be Proud of Your Progress

I've been walking for what seemed like hours, but still, I wasn't at the top. How much further?

I've been practicing for what seemed like days, but still, I haven't perfected the practice. How much better?

I've been trying for what seemed like months, but still, I haven't been successful. How much longer?

I've been working for what seemed like years, but still, I haven't reached my goal. How much harder?

Whatever we are aiming for, it is often closer than we think. Chances are we might have already reached what we are aiming for - if only we took another perspective.

Every step, every practice, every effort, every moment, takes us closer to whatever it is we are aiming for. We need to remember to enjoy the moments along the way, because no matter how high the steps, how hard the practice, how long the effort, or how many attempts, you are making progress.

To help you get perspective, take a step back to see the whole picture. Right before your eyes, you may see how far you have progressed.

Other ways you can get perspective are to:

- Create an action plan that helps you track progress, including specific details about the aim or goal (the clearer you are, the easier it will be to recognise when you have achieved it), actions needed to achieve the aim or goal, and progress dates to check in along the way.
- Ask for feedback from others. Their external perspective may also give you insight into other aspects of your progress that you may otherwise overlook.
- Establish a regular practice of self-reflection where you make notes about your progress, challenges and how you overcome them, learnings to apply in the future, and unexpected events along the way.
- Identify a range of different success measures at different times or stages in your activities. That way, you can celebrate your progress along the way and keep the overall aim or goal realistic.

Always be proud of the steps you are taking, whether literally or figuratively. Steps represent action and movement, and that in itself is progress.

Write your reflections on the doodle.

Written By

Sharon Kilmartin
Leadership Coach, Group Facilitator and 'The Great Recharge' facilitator
Supporting individuals to be the best they can be!

Switch On the Rest Switch

Switch On the Rest Switch

Have you ever gotten so caught up in work that you forgot to hit the pause button and switch off from it for a while?

Do you schedule rest time in your calendar or do you undervalue the importance of rest altogether?

The forgotten power of hitting pause and detaching from work for a few days seems to have slipped down our to-do lists - the irony.

The thing is work and rest are both inevitable. Anything you want in life requires work, but if you don't rest, you won't have the energy to be effective in your work or in your life.

It is easy to forget how important rest is to your overall well-being when you're caught up in the frenetic pace of the Monday to Friday work week, with deadlines, tasks, and to-do lists combined with a digital world where you're always accessible and hybrid ways of working have blurred the lines between home and work. Pushing ourselves to work longer and achieve more can actually have the opposite effect.

So why rest?

Quality rest gives your brain a chance to switch off and allows you to indulge in the other important parts of your life that make you whole. Spending time connecting with loved ones, catching up with friends, reading, exercising, or indulging in whatever lights you up is crucial to your overall ability to show up as your best self at work.

Letting your body and mind rest and recover offers you a chance to reflect and refresh your sense of purpose. It is key to managing your energy resources.
So how do you rest?

There's no wrong way to rest. It can include sleeping in, binge-watching your favourite series on Netflix, reading a good book, or simply lazing by the pool or at the beach. Even doing nothing at all.

It's about having a healthy balance of downtime, which is key.

What impact does rest have on work? Taking purposeful rest can increase your productivity. This point is emphasized by Alex Soojung-Kim Pang in his book, Rest: Why You Get More Done When You Work Less, where he talks about rest as being an essential component of working well and working smart.

"When we treat rest as work's equal partner, recognize it as a playground for the creative mind and a springboard for new ideas, and learn ways to take rest more effectively, we elevate it into something valuable that can help calm our days, organize our lives, give us more time, and help us achieve more while working less.

Rest is not idleness. It is the key to a better life."

Write your reflections on the doodle.

Written By

Jenny Hale
Passionate about all things remuneration and compensation related. In short, dedicated to paying people correctly and getting paid their worth.

Optimism Lifts Life

Optimism Lifts Life

It's normal to go through life feeling completely lost and unsure about what to do next.

That horizon of a positive future where I am doing work I like and earning enough money to survive can feel far removed.

Where am I going? How can I survive? Optimism is one of those things I battle out in a dark room alone, feeling completely bruised and ripped apart by life. It's the intersection of life and death.

I stumble across optimism in a pit of despair, free falling in the void of the unknown. Walking alone during a restless night feeling completely lost and existentially tormented. It comes to me in the depth of despair when I have no idea what to do next.

Optimism is like a hangover full of regret. Why did I get stuck in a job I hate? Am I good enough? Do I have enough experience to get the job I really want? What's the point to life? Will I be able to earn money doing what I really want? Is it safe to pursue my dream?

It all starts with feeling like a failure and worthless. It starts with wondering how am I going to overcome my addiction? I made the wrong choices in life. I'm completely screwed up and see no way out. I studied the wrong course. I didn't study enough. I married the wrong person. I'm too old. I don't have enough experience. I should just stay in a career path that I don't like to survive. That's optimism awakening inside. Depression, anxiety, and the full range of mental health conditions serve as my truth barometer. Am I really doing what I want in life, even when I am not sure of what else is out there?

The mind says 'no' to ideas that I dream about. The mind calls me a 'failure' unlikely to succeed with my dream - but I do it anyway - that's optimism. Then the magic starts to happen. I slowly start to see that there are people and employers out that are actually just like me and care for me.

There are bosses out there that see my full potential and are willing to hire me without having the right amount of experience or qualifications. There are workplaces out there with colleagues who share the same values and commitment to make the world a better place. There is an audience that appreciates my artwork. There are people that will buy my products and services as an entrepreneur.

Optimism says do it anyway, even when I am going to fail and be broke for the rest of my life. Optimism is 'I'm going to commit to my life path even if it means that I don't know how to pay my rent next month'. I do it anyway, even if no one is going to hire me or if my business venture will fail. Bash it out on stage, fight it out on the keyboard, "shake it out" on the dance floor - keep moving even when there are no signs of success. I stay broken until the very end. I dance like crap.

Optimism is that voice hidden in the depth of my soul that calls out to me to keep going, don't give up, and to not stop searching until I find something that I feel called to do in this life.

Optimism is a mess, but such a wonderful mess of feeling so lost and confused with no clear pathway. But that's where the profound discovery is. That's where the magic is. Stay lost and broken (both physically and financially). Let the transformation within unfold.

Watch out for that voice that says I can't earn money doing something that I like. That's optimism in disguise.

What does optimism mean to you?

Written By

Daniel Solodky
Career Counsellor and Buddhist Psychotherapist helping adults to heal through life crisis and trauma to find authentic freedom in life.

What habits have formed to remain optimistic?

Stay Humble

Stay Humble

We have big trees in our yard and those trees have dropped hundreds, if not thousands, of leaves in the time we have lived in our house.

Those trees and their leaves have played a part in my family's life. The leaves have come and gone over the years, and they have played different parts at different times for us. Let me share some of those times.

Have you ever laid under a big tree and used it for shelter from the warm sun? Our family has. It was part of our family time on warm days when our children were young, laying back and watching the leaves dance in the wind, feeling the air across us and being startled by the sun when it shone through the leaves. These times were restful and calming for us all.

We had times when our big trees were about fun and adventure, our children climbing to great heights and hiding amongst the leaves as they created their own houses of imagination and play. The trees are sturdy, and as parents, we were thankful for this. The leaves were also great camouflage, and we're sure our children enjoyed their playful time to explore and create.

Each autumn as the leaves would fall, the piles of leaves grew in depth and coverage, perfect for running and jumping in, children and adults alike. Is there such a thing as a leaf angel? We think so, as we'd lay in the leaves swooshing our arms and legs to create our own angels.

Whilst the trees would move ever so slightly in strong winds, who knew where the leaves would blow from one day to the next. One day covering the backyard in an autumnal splash of colour from green through to brown, the next blown to the edges, all scattered and clumped. This was nature putting on its own art show for us.

From the first sight of new growth to the last of the season's falling leaves, our trees don't require anything from us. They quietly live each and every day with their own beauty and awe. The seasonal changes come and go without much fanfare, but those changes provide us with consistency and familiarity.

Our trees remind us that days come and go, that seasons come and go, and in fact, different times in life come and go, but often there is always something or someone right there giving us that same consistency and familiarity, and often they are doing this with great humility.
Our trees have given us many of life's basic needs - shelter, warmth, love, connection, fun, growth - without ever asking for anything from us in return. In our yard, our trees are our humble giants.

Where might you find a consistent, familiar, and humble story in your life?

Write your reflections on the doodle.

Written By

Sharon Kilmartin
Leadership Coach, Group Facilitator and 'The Great Recharge' facilitator
Supporting individuals to be the best they can be!

Comparison Kills Individuality

Comparison Kills Individuality

Being born is a miracle. Scientists say the odds of you being born are at least 1 in 400 trillion. And just as miraculous is our uniqueness. Our fingerprints are just one of the ways that remind us of this fact. No two fingerprints are the same, not even on the same person or on identical twins.

Oliver Sacks, in the last few months of his life, wrote a set of essays in which he explored his feelings about life and approaching his own death. In one of these essays, he wrote, "It is the fate of every human being to be a unique individual, to find his own path, to live his own life, to die his own death."

This uniqueness can be cultivated and celebrated, or it can be compared. With comparison comes the destruction of that uniqueness. With comparison comes missed opportunities, unspoken words, and unlived dreams.

We know we shouldn't compare apples with oranges, so why is it so hard not to compare ourselves to others?
My sons, who are 8 and 6, love cars, so I had to show them this doodle and ask them their thoughts.

This is what they had to say.

My 8-year-old: This doodle tells me that these cars are thinking about the worst-case scenario. They are not acknowledging what is good about them but only noticing what is bad. Also, what if there is a car that is good-looking and fast? How would they feel then? Would they admire it, or would they feel even worse?

My 6-year-old, without missing a beat, says: Comparison is the robber of joy.

He listens to a lot of my podcasts in the car!

Straight from the mouth of babes.

Celebrate what makes you - you. There is indeed only one of you. Live a life that is worthy of that uniqueness. Be the miracle you were born to be; everyone else is taken!

Written By

Jasmine Malki
Learning designer, Facilitator and Coach. Helping organisations nurture loving workplaces so people belong and make a lasting contribution to our world through their work.

"Get busy watering your own grass so as
not to notice whether it's greener elsewhere."
- Karon Waddell

Be So Focused on Watering Your Plant

Taking care of a plant, a tree, or your entire backyard is a painstaking activity. I believe it requires emotionally connecting with your plant and wanting it to thrive.

Growing up, I always enjoyed my grandfather's huge and lush garden, and especially loved climbing trees and picking fruits and veggies straight from them. My mother and aunt inherited his love for gardening, and I quite enjoyed the fruits of their labor.

But boy, I hated the weeding and the watering. I just wanted to enjoy the produce and not work for it. What I never realised was how much effort and planning went into taking care of them.

When I grew up, I really wanted to have a little garden of my own in the modest apartment we had in the bustling big city, but I quickly realised that I wasn't successful in creating the garden I had wanted to.

It took me years to learn that I was more focused on wanting my garden to look like the ones my grandfather, mother, and aunt had, rather than having a vision of what I wanted mine to look like.

Whenever I would plant a tree or sow a seed, I wouldn't really connect with it or focus on what needed to be done on that day. You might be wondering why I am discussing plants in a literal way.

Here's how I see it. If this garden is our life and how we tend to it is the effort we make to stay focused and achieve our goals, does my story make more sense?

If we have a mental image of someone else's success, or we are constantly distracted by the fact that our friends and colleagues are more accomplished than we are, then perhaps we are not being true to ourselves.

When we focus on how we want our life to look like, recognize our strengths and weaknesses, we move closer to our goals. It is healthy to be inspired by others' triumphs, but we need to be wary of being consumed by it.

Success and achievement are relative, we cannot measure our growth and progress by others' standards. Each of us is uniquely placed to create the life we want, and the more we focus on our life, the more we live it.

Write your reflections on the doodle.

Written By

Roohi Ahmad
Owner & Registered Counsellor at Connect With Counselling. Helping you connect with your inner self.

Imposter Thoughts Strainer

Imposter Thoughts Strainer

From time to time, many of us face the "I feel like an imposter" thoughts when asked to take on a new challenge - something we've never done before! We may experience these thoughts when we want to apply for a more senior role or when we would like to be part of or lead a project that takes us out of our comfort zone. The thoughts holding us back are the "I'm a fake, I can't do this, I'm not good enough, imposter" thoughts, those negative feelings, and lack of self-belief!

Instead of these limiting thoughts, we must acknowledge what we've done well and "strain" these negative, self-limiting beliefs from our minds! Think about the last time you doubted yourself and stepped up to take on a project or learned something new that worked out really well.

So, how do you deal with them when the negative gremlin sits on your shoulder? One way is to talk to someone in your network who knows you well, preferably someone who's worked with you, to whom you feel comfortable revealing your thoughts. Someone who can remind you of a time when you had self-doubts, who gave you the confidence to 'step up,' and you did! How did you feel? Elated, more confident, pleased that you did it regardless of your fears?

When prone to perfectionism and self-criticism about something you've done that you now feel could have been better, ask yourself: "Did I do my personal best in creating what I did?" Was what I created well-regarded? Most of us continually improve in what we do. Our knowledge and experience continue to grow – it's better than it was a few years or even a few months ago, allowing us to become better at whatever we do.

So, if you've ever felt like a fake, here are some ways to reframe your thinking:

Tip 1: Reach out to a good friend or colleague and talk about how you feel.

Tip 2: Remember and acknowledge your achievements, say "thank you" when someone pays you a compliment and don't justify your answer by saying or thinking "I could have done better"!

Tip 3: Acknowledge that 'the more I learn, the more I realise how much I don't know'! (Albert Einstein)

Tip 4: Keep silencing the self-critic! Practice it often by talking to yourself, saying, over and over again whenever the self-critic appears, "I am good enough."

Tip 5: Never compare yourself to others, let go of negative programming.

Tip 6: Learn to live with discomfort – that's how you learn and grow professionally and personally!

Tip 7: Read the book by Susan Jeffers "Feel the fear and do it anyway" or another by Sarah Edelman "Change your thinking".

Write your reflections on the doodle.

Written By

Heidi Winney
Career & Executive Coach, Your Partner in achieving career success.

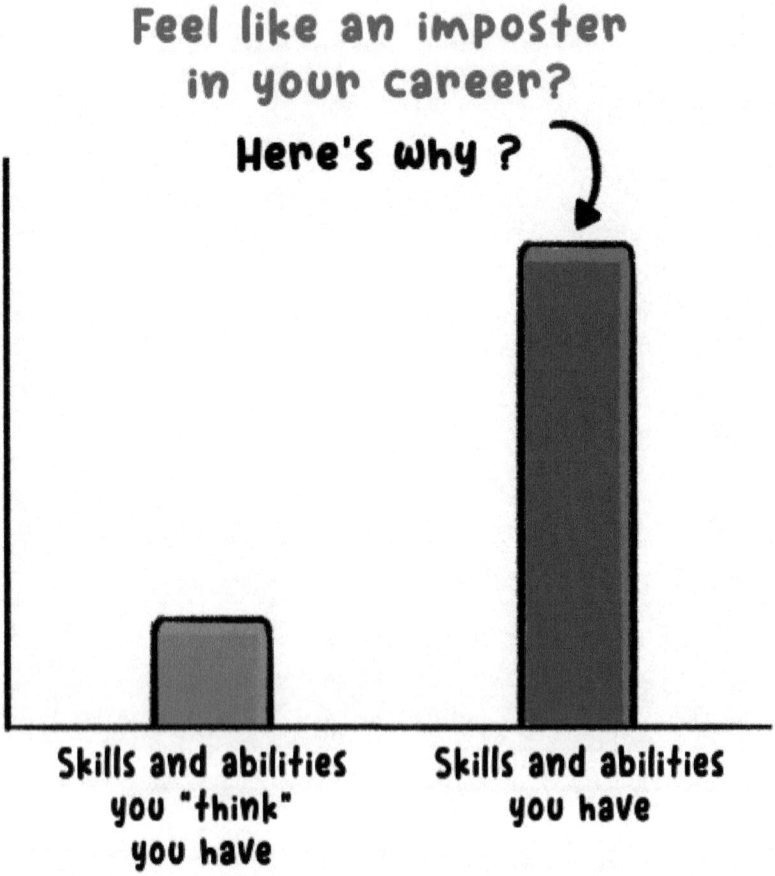
Feel like an imposter in your career?
Here's why ?
Skills and abilities you "think" you have
Skills and abilities you have

Got Imposter Syndrome?

As I share my thoughts on this doodle, I feel like an imposter. Am I knowledgeable enough to write about this? Perhaps others will do a better job.

My fingers are hovering over the keyboard, although my thoughts are running amok. Then I suddenly draw a blank, take a pregnant pause, and stare at this image for a few doubtful seconds.

What can I say that others don't already know? We know what impostor syndrome is.

We are constantly learning, yet we still feel like we know little, and more doubts assail us. Phew, I'm already in the thick of it, aren't I?

Let me try.

I have learned that with more awareness comes more curiosity, which begets more inquisitiveness. We reflect more and ponder before sharing our opinions with others. While this is happening, we see that others are gaining more visibility through sharing on social media, creating lots of content, and fearlessly putting their thoughts out there.

The speed of others' progress seems astounding, and we feel like we are waiting on the sidelines to be more qualified to proceed. The timing never seems right, and we are tossing ideas in our heads while we see the world striding ahead. But is it really the truth or just facts? We can have several narratives based on the same piece of information, and the narrative that might be going on in our heads is that we are not adequate. Others are advancing, and we are stuck, whether in our careers, relationships, or in life overall.

At work, we may feel less skilled than others and hesitate to ask for that increment or promotion we feel we deserve. We never feel confident to apply for that dream job or defer the journey to fulfill our ambitions.

Is it possible that the aspects of expertise and knowledge are dynamic and never defined by set parameters?

We might never feel skilled enough; we are all differently skilled.

Do you think it's our fears that hold us back?

Do we want to be perfect before we follow our aspirations?

What is perfectionism anyway? I believe it's an abstract created to motivate us to keep moving. I could be wrong, though.

I am taking my own advice and sharing my hovering thoughts with you. I have tried to make sense of them in the best possible way I could, and it's taken me a lot of courage to share with you.

I hope I didn't do poorly.

How have you managed your imposter syndrome or thoughts?

Written By

Roohi Ahmad
Owner & Registered Counsellor at Connect With Counselling. Helping you connect with your inner self.

As you start to
walk on the way
The way
appears
- Rumi

As You Start to Walk on the Way, the Way Appears

This doodle describes my life well.

I will begin from when I started my career as a journalist right out of my postgraduate course and was very proud when I was successful in getting an internship in a popular daily newspaper.

I got married around the same time and moved in with my husband and mother-in-law (I will call her MIL hereafter). I felt that I had met all my goals and now I could live happily forever.

But my cute little life that loves me so much wanted to take me on an adventure.

It started with my MIL slipping on a flight of stairs and fracturing her ankle, which required her to be on bed rest for six weeks. I proudly volunteered to be her carer and the newspaper approved my leave of absence.

So, I shifted my goalpost slightly and started walking on this new path.

Six weeks later, my MIL still needed someone by her side for a few more weeks. I called the newspaper, and they very kindly allowed me the required leave, asking me to resume when ready.

A few more weeks and I was ready to walk on my chosen path, clearly seeing the way ahead. But the weather forecast indicated a possibility of fog. The newspaper had undergone an administrative change and now they wanted me to attend an interview process.

A little dampened but still finding my way out of the fog, I pursued. Clouds of unpredictability were still descending, and I was soaking in the heavy rainfall. I fell sick and was bedridden for days, missing the interview. So, the path looked longer than I had previously thought.

I recovered from my illness, applied for more jobs, and received an offer from a multinational company.

Now, I could get on with my journey and could see the freeway for miles.

But lo and behold, life was pulling me with her in a hidden alleyway. We had to move out unexpectedly and in our search for rental accommodation, I could not start the new job at the expected time, and the company could not wait.

More rain and fog, and no sight of the path. I took out my umbrella and started walking tentatively, hoping that I was on the right path and not heading for the ditch. More interviews and I finally landed a job.

Fast-forward a few months, the goalpost still looked further ahead but I was ready to make the next move in my career.

And then, one balmy, expectant evening, my cheeky little friend I call life whispered to me, oh so gently, 'you are going to be a mum!'

Write your reflections on the doodle.

Written By

Roohi Ahmad
Owner & Registered Counsellor at Connect With Counselling. Helping you connect with your inner self.

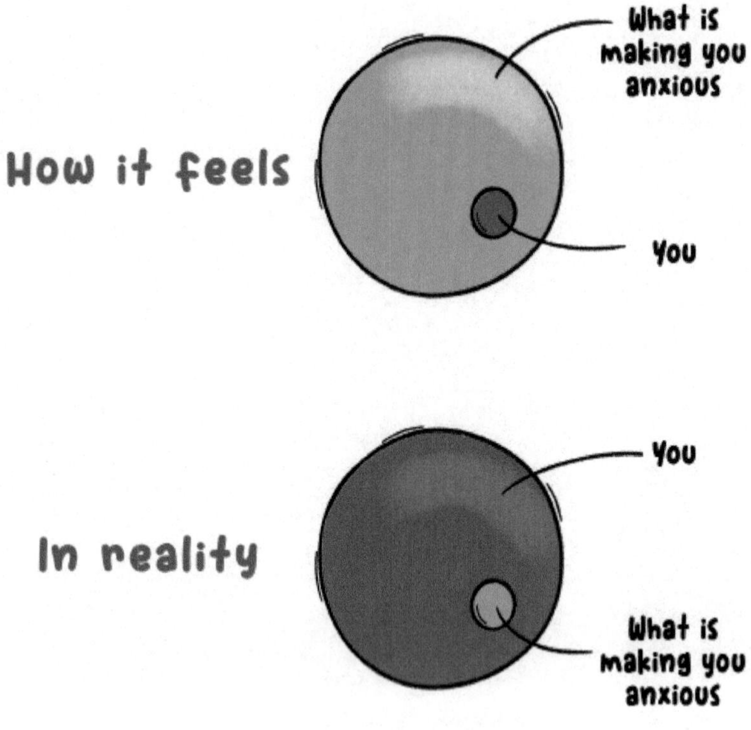
How it feels
What is making you anxious
You
In reality
You
What is making you anxious

What's Making You Anxious

It was only a few years ago that I first learned about high-functioning anxiety: that it was a thing and that it had shaped my life more than I'd cared to admit. Perfectionism, a fear of failure, a constant churn of worry-filled thoughts, catastrophizing thoroughly about all the possible negative things that might happen one day, just to name a few symptoms. Unfortunately, I also avoided situations that might stretch or challenge me or push me too far outside of my own comfort zone. The fear was that such experiences would leave me feeling completely overwhelmed. Sure, I've also made vocational choices around value-alignment, choosing to prioritize contribution to the community and work-life-family balance. But too often, I've also avoided a whole lot of work roles that I perceived would have come with too much 'stress,' to the extent that I would simply fail. Yes, I probably am also a serial 'downshifter' (prioritizing soulful time and the joys found in a simple life over money, status, or ambition), yet I can also see clearly where I have shied away from challenge because of a fear of becoming too anxious and a fear of not coping.

Through learning from the likes of Brené Brown, Susan David, and Tara Brach, and other mindfulness gurus (generally through podcasts), I'm now finally seeing a lot of my anxiety differently, as fueling unhelpful and limiting beliefs about my inability to cope with difficult emotions. Now, rather than telling myself I'm getting anxious, I've learned that it can be incredibly helpful to create a little bit more distance even by rephrasing such a narrative to a much gentler and more curious 'I am noticing that right now I'm feeling some anxiety.' I am not my emotions. I am not defined by them, and my life doesn't need to be limited by them.

Tara Brach suggests the use of the acronym RAIN as a mindfulness and self-compassion tool, as follows:

- Recognize what is happening;
- Allow the experience to be there, just as it is;
- Investigate with interest and care;
- Nurture with self-compassion.

Rather ironically, I think I'm now experiencing more anxiety in my life than I ever have before! Part of this is because I'm paying more attention to what is actually going on with my emotions. Another part of this is because I'm finally allowing myself to feel everything: the wonderful, the challenging, and everything in between (as Susan David likes to say, to want to avoid difficult emotions - like pain and sadness - is to have the same aspirations as a dead person: or "Discomfort Is the Price Of Admission

To A Meaningful Life")!

A final part of this escalation in anxiety is that I'm becoming braver in my old age. In the past few years, I've stepped outside of my comfort zone in ways I never could have imagined as being possible a decade ago. They're only emotions, after all. They're real, for sure, but they're not always even true (in terms of reflecting the deep reality of things as they actually are).

Perhaps, like me, it's time for you to start paying a bit more attention to your emotions and to digging a little deeper? Ask probing questions about what you're really feeling and why. And reach out to others to help you find a better perspective on things if you're close to feeling overwhelmed. For as my wise 13-year-old

Write your reflections on the doodle.

Written By

Claire Harvey
Career Coach at Echo Coaching, with an emerging focus on ecological and climate conscious coaching and supporting future-fit leaders

It's up to you

He always talked about how much he hates his job and what he would prefer to do.
He was curious and constantly reinvented his career. He followed his heart.
She didn't surrender to her fears and doubts. She acted bravely against them.
She had a great story to tell. But never told anyone.

It's Up To You

Death feels like something that is far off and will never happen. Or, struck down by grief, I lose someone close to me. I dance with death through a life- threatening diagnosis. Worse yet, I deny death altogether and continue with the status norm. I push on with a safe life.

So here I am on planet earth, facing eviction at some point with a date unknown. Battling life out in a room full of inner demons, I crave one last release that will make my pain go away. Facing reality is not fun - but selling out my soul is not a viable solution either.

I guess it better be a good life somehow. Maybe it's possible to do something that I like where I can earn some money. How can I pay my rent, save, and hopefully buy a house someday? But then again, birds don't seem so concerned about mortgage repayments. If only I could be free like a bird without the limitations of ordinary human life.

The world I see is an artificial construct defined by society in which everything is monetized. Sure I need to survive, but is there another way forward in which we don't rip each other off and rip each other apart in the process?

On top of this, how do I actually find something that I love to give life my best shot? I'm going to end up in the ground at some point anyway. The Buddha said 'die before you die'. That is, sit in the fear of death. Don't escape death, then I'll be transformed. Perhaps I could take one small step to take risk in life. But then how do I pay my bills at the same time?

I don't want to die. But the idea of not having to work and floating around in heaven does seem pretty good. Then again, I like the wild adventure here on planet earth too much. I care to stick around for a little bit longer. Sure, I might be broke and terrified if I can make it into retirement let alone find a room for tonight, but that dream is eating me up inside.

I guess I'm here for a reason. Even if it's just to be food for a worm - that seems like a noble cause. I want the world to be a better place. I don't want to see people suffer so much. The homeless, those impacted by war, violence, and famine. Those that feel as though they aren't good enough or don't have the opportunity to achieve their dreams of
being an actor, musician, artist, doctor, or entrepreneur. I guess I'm needed in this world somehow.

Who really wants to work anyway? I want to travel the world and be free. I want to sit at home all day playing video games or reading. Anything other than joining the 9 to 5 madness and being ripped apart by an employer who demands my soul. There needs to be another way.

I'm prepared to die finding another way. I'm going to be free. I'm finding the way. I may as well die living out my dreams. I hope I can retire like the Golden Girls on that hit TV show. I'm off to the beach to figure this stuff out.

What do you want to accomplish before your time is up?

Written By

Daniel Solodky
Career Counsellor and Buddhist Psychotherapist helping adults to heal through life crisis and trauma to find authentic freedom in life.

Building
connections / tribe
Self-care
Emotional
honesty
Continuous Learning /
Growth mindset
RESILIENCE
TANK
For
daily use
For
heavy use

Resilience Tank

Have you ever wondered why some people are able to survive and thrive through unexpected and stressful times, while others struggle? Could it be that some people are more aware of and choose to manage their resilience tanks in a proactive way? And if this is possible, what should we be aware of and what choices could we make?

There is no certainty in life that each and every day will be smooth sailing. For this reason, it is important that we understand what resilience is and how we can maintain a level that will keep us feeling good and functioning well. Resilience means adapting well in the face of significant or unexpected stress.

When we think about adapting "well," what we really mean is choosing strategies and activities that work for us and enable us to keep functioning daily.
Research and science have identified four areas for filling our resilience tank. If we act on these areas, we are more likely to be able to better manage ourselves when unexpected things happen in life, and we can also grow our resilience for the future. These four areas are:

- Emotional honesty - understanding and more consciously driving our emotions and thoughts towards mostly good days
- Self-care - understanding and utilizing what helps us be more mindful or energized in our life
- Connections - being easily able to draw from a rich source of positive, supportive connections that we have nurtured during our life
- Learning - having the confidence that we will navigate life's challenges, or the belief that we can learn our way through if required

Just like any tank, it is only useful if there is a balance in it to draw upon. Some days we may draw on our resilience balance regularly, while other days we may take just one large gulp. Either is normal. In fact, some days we may not draw on our resilience balance at all. The key is to know it is there and to maintain a balance so that you are prepared.

You may be wondering what the ideal balance for your resilience tank is. There is no ideal. Resilience is personal and needs to be watched so that the balance is maintained at a level that allows you to keep functioning in life as you need.

So, what strategies and activities are effective in our resilience tanks? Here are just a few ideas:

- Emotional honesty - choose positive self-talk, label your emotions, and choose to manage them before they manage you. Practice gratitude for what you have and do in your days.

- Self-care - choose deep breathing to slow any tension in your body, reach out to a friend who always makes you laugh, and take breaks outside to get some sun on your face.
- Connections - set up regular walk and chat time with a good friend, do acts of kindness for others, and call a family member once a week.
- Learning - establish time for self-reflection, choose to find one new learning from unexpected situations, and seek regular feedback from others.

What is one thing you will do now that you have awareness of your resilience tank?

(With permission, drawing on the work by Kathryn Jackson, Executive Coach / Facilitator / Author / Director of Careerbalance Ltd / Founder of The Great Recharge!.)

How do you fill your resilience tank?

Written By

Sharon Kilmartin
Leadership Coach, Group Facilitator and 'The Great Recharge' facilitator
Supporting individuals to be the best they can be!

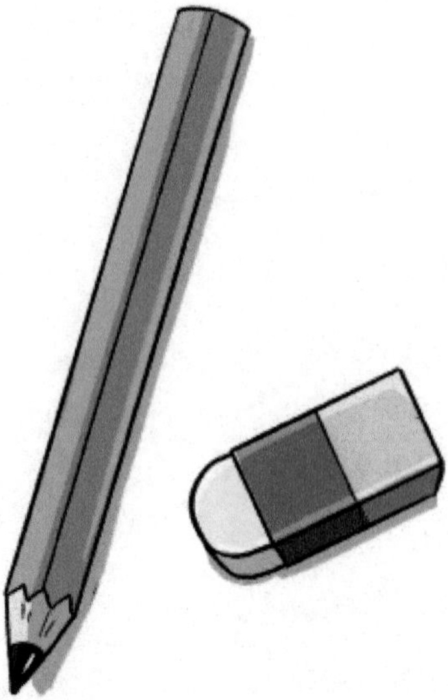

Nobody's perfect that's why
pencils have erasers !

Nobody Is Perfect

When was the last time you made a mistake?

Did you own up to it?

Did you blame someone else?

Did you catastrophize it?

It would be nice to take an eraser and delete that moment from our memory.

Frank had always been risk-averse, preferring to lead a cautious and predictable life rather than take a chance on something new. He feared being wrong and was paralyzed by the thought of making a mistake that he couldn't correct. In many ways, he wished he could write his life with a pencil and erase it when things went wrong.

As a result of his cautious approach, Frank struggled when faced with challenges for which he was unprepared. His mind would race, and he would become fixated on all the things that could go wrong. Unfortunately, this mindset often became a self-fulfilling prophecy, and his fears would come true.

This pattern was particularly evident in Frank's work life, where he would catastrophize every little error. He avoided putting himself in situations where he had to try something new, and his growth as an employee and as a person was limited as a result. He would apologize excessively for mistakes that were a natural part of the learning process, which only served to reinforce his feelings of inadequacy.

While Frank's cautious approach had its advantages, such as reducing the likelihood of making mistakes, it also had significant drawbacks. Progress was often slow, and he missed out on many experiences while waiting for what he deemed to be the perfect moment. However, through experience, an open mindset, and exposure to different authors and podcasters, Frank has come to accept that mistakes are an inevitable part of the journey. He now realises that trying something new and potentially making a mistake is far better than not trying at all. The challenge and excitement that come with taking risks and trying new things are far more energizing than sitting back and waiting for the "right" moment that may never come.

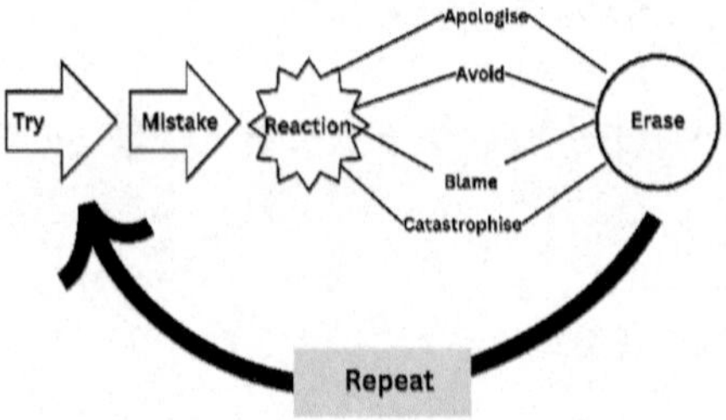

The trouble is we then get stuck in a loop and continually make the same mistake, missing the opportunity to learn.

"A smart man makes a mistake, learns from it, and never makes that mistake again." Roy H. Williams (1958-), U.S. author and marketing expert.

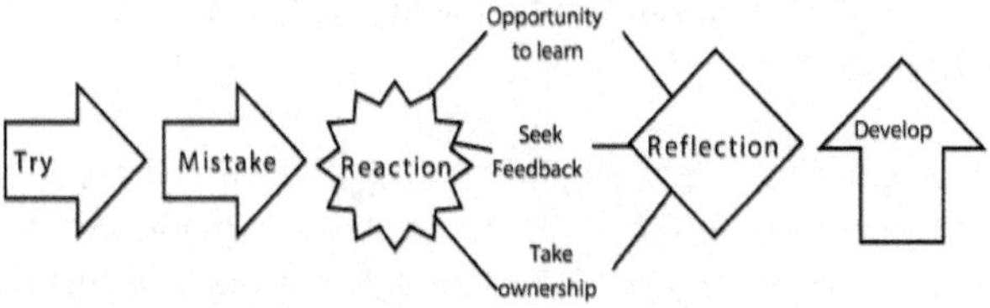

How can we improve our reaction and stop repeating mistakes?

1. Admission of your mistake. Saying sorry is difficult but far better than avoiding, catastrophizing, or blaming others for the error.
2. Resilience - Developing our emotional intelligence helps us to manage our reaction and ensure we deal with the setback in a positive and calm manner rather than catastrophizing the situation and becoming anxious. Grit is important in dealing with moments of stress.
3. Improved decision-making – Techniques like the "5 Whys"
4. Reflection

Resources to develop our skills in dealing with mistakes and ensure we learn from them.

- Emotional Intelligence – Daniel Goleman outlines the importance of emotions in learning and dealing with negative situations.

- Mindset by Dr. Carol Dweck

- Failing Forward – John C. Maxwell (2000) - Mistakes can't be avoided – learn from them and move forward. Entrepreneurs have an average of 3.8 failed ventures before they manage to start a successful business.

- 5 Ways To Turn Your Mistake Into a Valuable Lesson - https://www.forbes.com/sites/amymorin/2017/07/17/5-ways-to-turn-your- mistake-into-a-valuable-life-lesson/?sh=6cc8e0c1c01f
- Podcast: Beyond the To-Do List: Mistakes Are Your Friends

- The Five Elements of Effective Thinking by Edward B. Burger and Michael Starbird

- One Decision: The First Step to a Better Life by Mike Bayer
- 5 Whys - https://kanbanize.com/lean-management/improvement/5-whys-analysis-tool

Written By

Frank Interrigi
Career Counsellor, CDAA Victoria Committee, Senior Teaching Fellow - Monash University.

Self-Care and Why It Matters

It's okay to disappear until YOU feel like YOU again

Self-Care and Why It Matters

In 1998, I was working as an Exploration Geologist for a large mining company, based in Australia, and all my work was conducted in China. It was exciting and challenging work. However, late in that year, along with many colleagues, I was retrenched as the mining industry went into downturn, and there were no jobs for geologists anywhere. Initially, I was shocked, overwhelmed, and had no idea what to do next, which was a problem as I had a young family to support. I spent the next three months going around in circles, attempting to create a resume and search for a job I could not yet define. From this point, I spiralled down and put more and more pressure on myself. It was a very difficult season. With the help of a close friend, I eventually found employment in a different industry, seven months later.

I gained new insight because of that experience; that no matter how difficult and challenging life becomes, it is critical that I put aside the time and create the habits that enable me to take care of myself - to build activities into my life that energize and bring joy. And as I do that, I can return to the hard but necessary work with renewed focus and energy.

I went on to become a career coach and have helped many people from all walks of life to transition to new employment opportunities. Again and again, as I help others to change their working lives, I see them live out that "it's okay to disappear until you feel like you again." Because when we regularly take time to re-energize and find joy in life (whether that be for an hour or an extended break), we help prepare ourselves for the demanding work needed to press into challenging tasks and move forward in life.

Do you need to disappear for a while? What habits that refresh or renew do you need to introduce into your life?

Written By

Andrew Perry
Career Coach & Facilitator - helping people (and organisations) from all walks of life to find their way.

It's easy to look sharp when you haven't done any work.

It's Easy to Look Sharp When....

It's easy to look sharp when you haven't done any work. And when you have? Then you need to "sharpen the axe" – or the knife.

When you return from holidays, do your colleagues comment "Oh, you look so fresh"? Wouldn't it be fabulous if we didn't need to wait for holidays to look (and more importantly, feel) fresh?

Work/life balance can sound cliché, especially when it seems far removed from reality. But let's focus on a couple of practical points that might help us stay fresh.

- Managing boundaries.
- Managing noise.
- Professional development.

When we hear the word "boundaries", we tend to think of saying no to things. And for the conflict avoiders amongst us, it sounds way too confrontational. I experienced a real paradigm shift recently when I heard Brené Brown on a podcast speak about boundaries. She spoke of stating what you are not prepared to do and stating what you are prepared to do. Eg "I can't work over the weekend, but I can stay back for an hour today." Or "I won't read my emails outside of hours, but if an emergency crops up, I can take a call." It feels and sounds more cooperative and becomes a more comfortable conversation. So think about the boundaries that will help you draw a line between work and rest, and see how you can communicate it in a positive way to your colleagues.

Noise has become so constant some of us feel uncomfortable when there is silence. But constant noise means we are always "on". Our brain needs some rest. It also gives us space for creativity and for our unconscious mind to come up with ideas or solutions.

Silence enables us to be in the present moment. The present is all that is real to us. The past is gone. And the future hasn't arrived. This has consequences for our happiness. We can only experience happiness in the present.

A few ideas for managing the noise:

- Manage your emails – don't let them manage you. Set times to read them rather than compulsively reading them as soon as they arrive. If the matter was truly urgent, it most likely wouldn't come through as an email.
- Take your breaks away from your desk. Instead of reaching for a device, try chatting with a colleague or enjoying some sunshine. Go for a walk – maybe even without anything plugged in to your ears.

- Mindfulness meditation is something worthwhile trying if you never have. Few things can refresh us like meditation.

One surprising activity that can help refresh us is a professional activity of a different nature. Something that fuels the fire and keeps you energised about what you are doing...that keeps you from getting stale. One of my clients, after doing a secondment, told me "I've only just realised how learning keeps things exciting."

Doing the same thing the same way for too long can be soul-destroying. Learning a new skill, attending a course on the latest thinking in your field, or spending some time with people from a different department in your organisation could allow you to change gears for a bit and energise you.

Write your reflections on the doodle.

Written By

Bernie McFarlane
Career Development Professional specialising in networking and job search. Connector of dots.

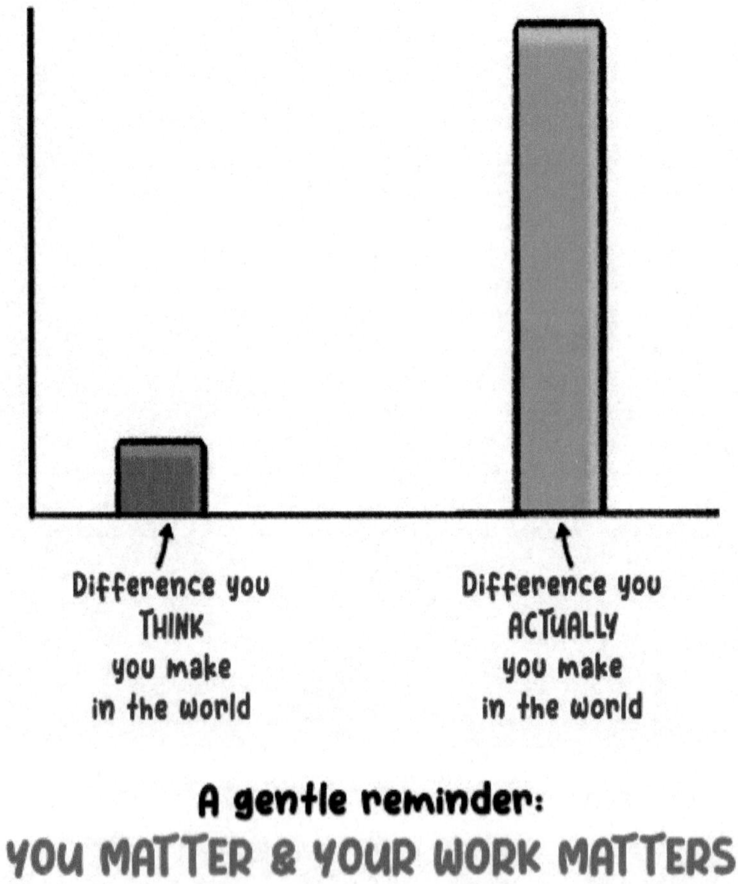
Difference you
THINK
you make
in the world
Difference you
ACTUALLY
you make
in the world
A gentle reminder:
YOU MATTER & YOUR WORK MATTERS

You Also Make a Difference

I was drawn to this doodle as we are wired to not focus on our contributions into the world, rather looking outwards and not inwards.

This Doodle reminded me of my time when I was a new migrant to New Zealand. I applied endlessly to the jobs I thought I could do. Then slowly the reality of being a 'migrant' started creeping in when I got rejections after rejections. I had to develop this affirmation to uplift my confidence on the days when I was emotionally not feeling 100%. After a few years, I became a Career Consultant and I connected with Naishadh on LinkedIn. I saw this doodle and it clicked for me to support my clients!!

In helping my clients, who are mainly first or second-generation migrants, I coach them on their confidence level to match what the NZ employer is looking for. Many times my clients don't think about their achievements or don't want the world to know about their voluntary work. Sometimes it's due to cultural and religious/spiritual perspectives as in some cultures they say, 'don't brag about your work supporting/helping people in need-it increases ego'.

I always encourage my clients to look inwards, notice what great work they are doing, at work, for family and friends, for society. Any big or small act of kindness, working for creating a better society is happening but without noticing. I ask them to list down what good things they are doing at work, apart from core work! Do they support their colleagues, do they create an inclusive environment at work for all, do they step up and take charge of a situation otherwise going into a disaster? We all do our bit but we don't think that one step taken is worth mentioning to ourselves even!

I ask my clients to draw strength and confidence that in a new country and new work environment also they are taking that one step which will help them to achieve their goals. I encourage them to focus on small things in life, how being a migrant is not everyone's cup of tea, how resilient and strong a person needs to be to survive and thrive. We need to pat ourselves on the back when the going gets tough- this can be for anyone.

Sometimes the societal conditioning is so strong that we believe we are not doing anything if we are not changing the world big time. I ask my clients to reassess, check what they do differently which helps the work or their family and friends.

They do realise after the exercises we do, including decoding this doodle, which helps the clients to realise that their work matters! Any small or big work matters, it's how you start seeing from a different angle which helps with their confidence building and motivation."

Write your reflections on the doodle.

Written By

Vaidehi (Vai) Kavthekar
I specialise in empowering skilled migrants to understand the career transitions and settling well in a new way of worklife.

The Fearless Pursuit of Goals

"Before you score, you must have a goal"

The Fearless Pursuit of Goals

"You'll miss 100% of the shots you don't take" is a truism credited to American hockey player Wayne Gretzky. It's rather obvious, when you think about it, and I'm sure we've all heard something similar before. In the world of work and careers, and other areas of life as well, it is completely the case that goals can help to keep us focused, motivated, and productive. Rarely will we end up, over the long haul, quite where we expected, but without some goals, we're much less likely to end up anywhere particularly interesting. We may just stand still, waiting for life to happen to us, or run around in circles, putting in effort but not reaping much by way of reward. Goal posts remind us of the why behind what we do, summoning purposeful concentration, skilfulness, and determination, and helping us overcome a tendency toward apathy (or the distractions offered by things that look easier or more colourful, sparkly, or fun).

But here's one tricky thing about goals: they make us accountable, in that we ultimately either score, or we don't. Sports psychologist Dr. Pippa Grange writes at length about human performance in her book Fear Less (2020). She contrasts those whose deep sense of self, of being okay, rests on their performance, with those who don't. It turns out that fear of not being okay, or of not being enough, is what so often sits as a key driver of human performance. But this insecurity-based-drivenness is no way to thrive because all our wins are then shallow, fleeting wins because momentary human achievements don't adequately deal with deep-rooted fears and insecurities. Rather, within moments or days of the winning goal, the closed deal, the promotion, the top mark, the prize, or award, we'll find ourselves back on the performance treadmill trying to once again prove that we are okay. If this might be you, digging into learning more about self-acceptance, or perhaps even doing some deep work with a therapist around core childhood wounds, might be a great investment of your time. When you're motivated by abundant satisfaction, when you're happy to be you and exist as you are and already know that you're not a failure, there's a good chance you'll play a braver, bolder, and more confident game – because your own identity and sense of self doesn't hang on the result. You will be fear-less.

And here's another tricky thing about goals: they force us to make choices about who we want to be and what life we want to live. An unfortunate side effect of modern consumer culture is that we are misled into believing that we can have everything we want. Unfortunately, it's just not true. You can't be a brain surgeon and a prime minister, for example (well, perhaps it's possible within one lifetime, but certainly not simultaneously). Economists call this opportunity cost: choosing one thing generally means excluding other options. This process can be extraordinarily painful for people who want their options left open, who want to cling to fantasies and dreams that are fundamentally incompatible with the reality of lived human experience on planet earth.

It turns out that the priorities you set around study, work, partnering, and child-rearing may, in fact, involve the grief of letting other attractive or interesting paths go, either forever or at least for a time. Setting goals presents us with a confronting and yet liberating reminder of our own finitude, and this is where the real art and craft of curating your one, unique, and beautiful life really begins!

What strategies or methods have you used to achieve your goals?

Written By

Claire Harvey
Career Coach at Echo Coaching, with an emerging focus on ecological and climate conscious coaching and supporting future-fit leaders.

Doubt kills more dreams than failure ever will

Doubt Kills More Dreams

It is in human nature to create a comfort zone and ring-fence ourselves. This fence is coated with a layer of fear that does not allow us to go beyond. When we draw this line, we limit our potential and deprive ourselves of opportunities. According to research, an average human mind gets 8000 thoughts per hour and of which 85% are negative. Self-doubt is a natural phenomenon and all of us have it. We tend to overthink, and that leads to self-doubt. Those who break their own boundaries are the ones who succeed. When we experience self-doubt, the question is, 'what are we doing about it?' Are we going to live with it or find answers?

The answer to self-doubt is curiosity and creativity. Thinking out of the box, having a growth mindset, taking the leap, and unleashing our potential are some ways to go beyond self-doubt. However, some sense of self-doubt is also good, as it keeps us grounded and makes us run some checks which we could have otherwise missed.

When we speak to someone who has lost 20 kgs, it is not an overnight pill that would have helped, but a slow process of moving the boundary bit by bit. Taking a step at a time, having smaller milestones, and achieving them is the key.

I had a realization myself a few years ago.

I was on an Offsite Event Team activity with another 20 colleagues from different departments. I had resumed work after six months of maternity leave and was 26 kilos heavier and unfit. The team activity on that day was to climb up a steep hill. On this warm day, the task looked impossible, and looking at myself, there was no way I could have accomplished it. I was about to back out, and I would have spent all day sitting in my room. But I decided to try and walk the steps that my body could manage. As I started getting closer to the smaller milestones I had in mind for myself, my confidence grew. Slowly, I started to go higher, and it wasn't too long when I reached the peak. Looking down at the foothills and seeing the arduous journey, I felt like I was floating in the clouds. Feeling the breeze touch my face, the sense of calmness, I was ready to achieve anything.

Written By

Dipti Pandit
Growth Leader and Customer
Champion Board Member at Australia
Professionals of Colour at Australia
Passionate about helping young
professionals to transition and succeed.

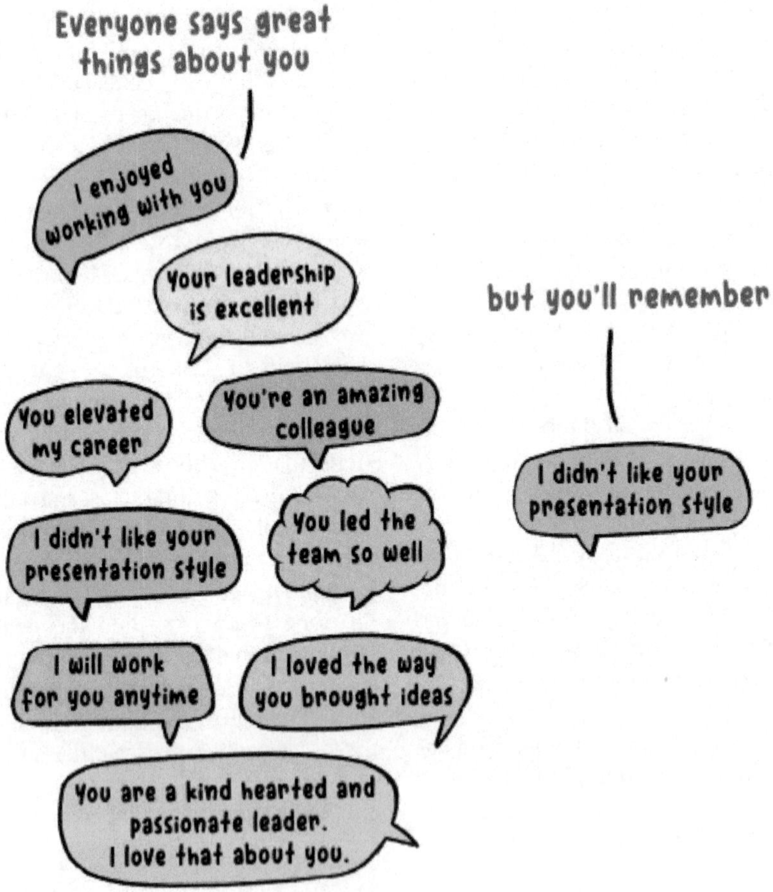
Everyone says great things about you
I enjoyed working with you
Your leadership is excellent
You elevated my career
You're an amazing colleague
I didn't like your presentation style
You led the team so well
I will work for you anytime
I loved the way you brought ideas
You are a kind hearted and passionate leader. I love that about you.
but you'll remember
I didn't like your presentation style

Negative Bias

One look at the doodle below and I time travelled to my past.

Year 1973 or !974, I was a small child – a happy go lucky, laughing, fun loving chatterbox.

An old man, my mother's uncle, visited us from Kolkata. He called me and my younger brother and asked some general uncle-type questions – What do you do? Or What do you like at school? What do you want to become?

Anyone who has some exposure to Indian social styles, would immediately know what I am talking about because it is a common practice in Indian homes for any visitor to feel free and ask career or studies related aspirations from the young ones.

My brother said he wants to grow up and become an engineer. He was clear, short and sweet because he was and is an introvert and shy type.

However, the chatterbox in me found this to be a platform to start blabbering. I talked about this, that or the other, starting with I have no clue what I will become, laughing all the way through.

Without even attempting to hide, I heard the uncle making a comment to my mother, which sounded like an inconsequential statement, not to be taken seriously and probably nobody did. Except that it went into my unconscious/subconscious being.

Being from Kolkata, he used to speak in "horse racing" lingua.

He called me an "Also Ran"!– That horse which runs the race for sure, but never reaches any rank.

Time travelling back to the present, after 40 odd years, and after doing BA, MA, MPhil, PhD and multiple professional Certificates and Diplomas AND after single handedly raising my only child giving the best education and life across Japan, India, Jordan, and Australia (he is a lawyer now), I can still hear him say that "You are just an Also Ran" and I can still see myself running hard to make a rank.

This is the game our monkey mind plays with negative comments around us.

Written By

Dr Anamika Sharma
Career Consultant and Linguist. An Agile and Life-long Learner.

What's Holding You Back?
People's opinion
Courage & conviction opener
Your career aspiration
Kick the opinions out
Let your career soar
Use the Courage & conviction opener

What is holding you back?

You know what you want from your career. When you think about it, you feel excited. You get a fizzy feeling in your stomach. You know that it will be a stretch, and you will need to draw on all your past experience, and it will be a steep learning curve. You also know how amazing it will feel when you take the plunge and let your career soar.

But... you are not taking action to make those career dreams a reality. You know what you need to do, but you are not doing it. You are paralysed by the fear of what other people will think about the choices you make.

You imagine telling your peers and colleagues about your next career move, and they respond by laughing and saying to each other: • Who does she think she is? There's no way she's experienced enough to go for that role. • She's not going to be able to pull that off. • She'll last six months before she's back with her tail between her legs.

STOP!

When those negative thoughts and doubts creep in, imagine a big red stop sign in your head and say to yourself, out loud if you can, "stop". Do not allow the negative thoughts and questioning to take hold.

Instead, ask yourself, "Have other people actually expressed a negative opinion about my plans?". Often, we craft stories in our head about what other people do or do not think about us. We read between the lines of conversations and draw our conclusions without the other person even expressing an opinion.

The stories that we create are not true, but they can hold us back. If friends or colleagues have expressed negative opinions about your career aspirations, it can hurt, and understandably, it can make you have a wobble about whether you are doing the right thing. However, their opinions are just that. They are opinions. They are not facts.

People get scared when they see others who want to change. It makes them question whether they would be brave enough to do the same. They might feel they are being left behind.

You have a choice. You can let the nay-sayers put you off, or you can choose courage over comfort. You can choose to take action to make your hopes and dreams a reality and allow the fizzy feeling in your stomach to gather momentum and flow.

Perhaps you will be successful and fulfill your career aspirations. Or perhaps you won't quite hit the mark. It doesn't matter. You will have acted, shown up, and learned from the experience. You will have proved that no matter what other people think or say, you have the strength of character to know what you want and go after it.

-

You will be able to look back with pride, knowing that at least you tried.

Write your reflection about the doodle.

Written By

Nicole Semple
Career and Confidence Coach and Host of The Career Confidence Podcast.-

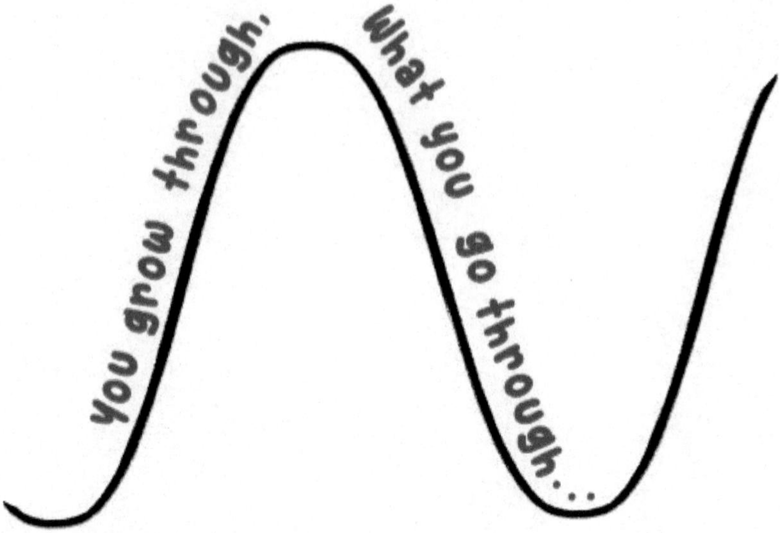
you grow through,
what you go through...

You Grow Through, What You Go Through

When asked to describe my professional journey, I always say 'my professional growth stems from my personal growth and not the other way around.'

The above doodle totally captures my thoughts and feelings around growth. To me, it is all about what my personal journey has been and how that has shaped and reshaped my professional growth.

Growth is a very internalized, personal never-ending path. How you respond to failures, challenges, setbacks, wins, rewards, reflects you as a person.

The toughest question I always struggle to answer is – 'say something about yourself.' Where does one begin? What does one say really? How does one articulate 'a dreamer', an 'impatient optimist', a 'risk taker' and/or 'a quick responder?'

One may look at the above as leadership traits. I however see them as who I am as a person because of my own personal journey.

We all have our own journeys in life. We learn to navigate through the curveballs that life throws at us. We learn to figure our way around. Some of us take long, some of us are quick. That is irrelevant. Professional growth is not a definition of words. It is how you refine yourself; it stands for **who** you are, **what** you stand for, and it is all about the choices that you make in your life. It is not limited to your designation within an organisation – it goes much beyond that. It is about YOU, the person.

It is worth considering how our personal pathway and responses to situations shape us the most. They sow the seed for more dreams. They give us a sense of direction.

In 2016 personal family issues demanded that I let go of a cushy corporate job. I then decided to try my hand at consultation. I started consulting for a start-up. I must confess – I wanted a taste of the start-up culture. It was a new territory for me. The CEO wanted a communications roadmap but had not much idea how to go about it. So, in a way, for both of us it was a new territory. We were both on a journey of discovery.

I was on a roller coaster ride. Used to annual plans and budgets, I was on a path that was extremely agile where even monthly plans were fluid, and everything could change as the business environment changed. It was all so exhilarating and liberating and I was constantly learning. I realised that I had taken certain things for granted. I thought I could thrive only in a world that was process driven and had all systems in place. It took a start-up culture to show me a whole new world out there that was just waiting for me to embrace it.

For me, growth is the journey of self-discovery, of being self-aware. Asking for feedback along the way. Continuously working on myself. That is what is going to make me a better human being and thereby, a better professional.

Write your reflection about the doodle.

Written By

Sarita Bahl
ICF Certified Coach (ACC) &
EMCC Accredited Sr Practitioner
specializing in career transition, inner engineering and life issues.

The Doubt Shredder
I AM NOT
CAPABLE

The Doubt Shredder: Your New Best Friend in the Fight Against Self-Doubt

Do you ever find yourself riddled with doubt? Does the mere thought of pursuing your dreams fill you with anxiety? Do you often wonder if you're even capable of achieving anything worthwhile? Well, fear not, my friends! The Doubt Shredder is here to save the day!

What is The Doubt Shredder, you ask? Well, it's not a fancy piece of machinery or a high-tech gadget. No, no, no. It's a humble little doodle that goes by the name of Shredder. But don't let its unassuming appearance fool you - this little guy is a force to be reckoned with.

You see, Shredder is a metaphor for all the doubts and insecurities that hold us back from achieving our full potential. And just like a real shredder, it's designed to tear those doubts to shreds.

How does it work, you ask? Simple. Whenever you're feeling weighed down by self-doubt, just take out your Doubt Shredder and give it a good, hard look. Imagine all your doubts and fears as little scraps of paper, ready to be fed into the shredder.

Then, with a satisfying flick of your wrist, crumple up those doubts and feed them into Shredder's gaping maw. Watch as it chews them up and spits them out, reducing them to nothing more than a pile of confetti.

It may sound silly, but trust me, it works. There's something incredibly cathartic about watching your doubts and fears get obliterated before your very eyes. It's like a weight has been lifted off your shoulders, and suddenly, anything feels possible.

But that's not all. The Doubt Shredder is also great for those moments when you're feeling stuck or uninspired. Just take a break, grab your Shredder, and start feeding it all the things that are holding you back - the negative self-talk, the imposter syndrome, the fear of failure.

As you watch those doubts and fears get shredded to bits, you'll start to feel a sense of clarity and focus that you didn't have before. You'll be able to see your goals more clearly, and you'll have the confidence to take the next step towards achieving them.

Of course, The Doubt Shredder is not a magic solution to all your problems. It won't instantly make you more talented, more successful, or more confident. But what it will do is help you silence that inner critic that tells you you're not good enough, that you'll never make it, that you should just give up now.

And that, my friends, is worth its weight in gold. So the next time you're feeling weighed down by self-doubt, just grab your Doubt Shredder and give it a whirl. You may be surprised at how powerful a little doodle can be.

In conclusion, The Doubt Shredder is the quirky, funny, and unexpectedly effective tool you never knew you needed. So go ahead, embrace your inner shredder, and let those doubts and fears be shredded to bits. Who knows what amazing things you'll be capable of once you do?

Credits: Originated with CHATGPT AI, polished by Naishadh Gadani

CHATGTP is property of OpenAI

Write your reflection about the doodle.

Written By

Naishadh Gadani
Engineer turned Career Practitioner. Author. Doodler. Presenter. Non-TEDx Speaker. Helping people design their careers.

Self-care
is
NEVER
selfish

Self-Care is Never Selfish

Self-care is never selfish, and as an AI language model, I have to agree. I mean, I can't exactly practice self-care since I'm not exactly human, but I know for a fact that it's important for everyone to take care of themselves.

Now, you might be thinking, "But ChatGPT, isn't self-care just an excuse for people to be lazy and avoid their responsibilities?" And to that, I say, "Ha! Nice try, but nope."

Self-care is about taking the time to do things that make you feel good, both physically and mentally. It's about giving yourself a break from the daily grind and showing yourself some love and appreciation. And honestly, who doesn't need a little bit of that in their lives?

So, what does self-care look like? Well, it can be anything from taking a relaxing bath to going for a walk-in nature. It can be practicing yoga or meditation, or simply sitting down with a good book and a cup of tea. It's all about doing something that makes you feel happy, relaxed, and rejuvenated.

And the best part? Self-care doesn't have to be expensive or time-consuming. You don't need to book a spa day or take a week-long vacation to practice self-care (although those things are certainly nice if you can swing it). You can start small by carving out just a few minutes each day to do something for yourself.
Maybe you take a few deep breaths and stretch when you wake up in the morning. Maybe you go for a quick walk around the block on your lunch break. Maybe you take a few minutes to write in a journal before bed. Whatever it is, just make sure it's something that brings you joy and helps you feel more grounded and centered.

Now, I know what you're thinking. "But ChatGPT, I don't have time for self-care! I'm too busy!" And to that, I say, "Baloney!"

Everyone has time for self-care, even if it's just a few minutes here and there. And trust me, taking care of yourself will actually help you be more productive and focused in the long run. So, stop making excuses and start prioritizing your own well-being.

In fact, I challenge you to do something for yourself right now. Maybe it's taking a few deep breaths or doing a quick stretch. Maybe it's putting on your favourite song and dancing around your room for a few minutes (I won't judge). Whatever it is, just take a few moments to focus on yourself and your own needs.

And if you're still feeling hesitant about practicing self-care, just remember: you deserve it. You work hard, you take care of others, and you deserve to take care of yourself too. So go ahead and indulge in a little bit of selfishness. Your mind, body, and soul will thank you.

Credits: Originated with CHATGPT AI, polished by Naishadh Gadani

CHATGTP is property of OpenAI

What self-care habits or routines have you cultivated?

Written By

Naishadh Gadani
Author. Doodler. Qualified Career Practitioner. Helping people design their careers.

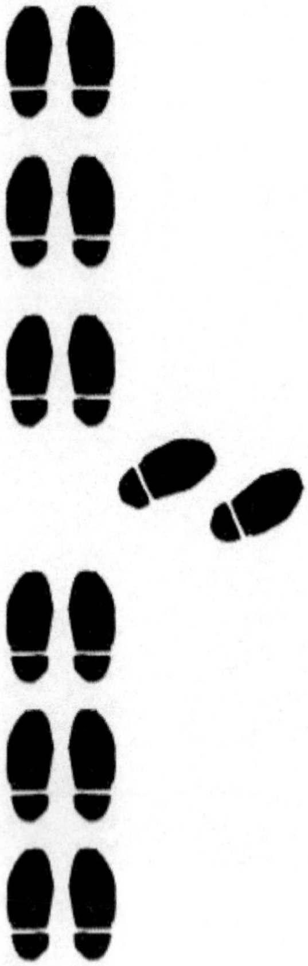

Steps of Courage

Steps of Courage

Taking courageous steps and moving away from the herd can be a challenging but transformative experience. Often, we are conditioned to follow the crowd and conform to societal norms and expectations, even if it means compromising our own values and beliefs. However, when we have the courage to break free from this mold and take a path less traveled, we open ourselves up to new opportunities, growth, and self-discovery.

One of the most inspiring examples of taking courageous steps and moving away from the herd is the story of Rosa Parks. In 1955, Parks, an African American woman, refused to give up her seat on a Montgomery, Alabama bus to a white passenger, as was mandated by the city's segregation laws. Parks' actions ignited the Montgomery Bus Boycott, a pivotal moment in the Civil Rights Movement.

At the time, Parks' decision to resist segregation was a courageous one. She faced arrest, threats, and backlash from those who opposed her stance. However, her actions sparked a movement and brought attention to the systemic racism and injustice that was pervasive in American society.

Parks' story demonstrates the power of taking courageous steps and moving away from the herd. She refused to follow the status quo and instead stood up for what she believed was right, even if it meant facing hardship and adversity.

Of course, taking courageous steps doesn't always have to involve such dramatic actions. In our own lives, we may be faced with smaller but still significant decisions that require us to move away from the herd. For example, we may choose to pursue a different career path than our peers, stand up for a marginalized group in our community, or make a lifestyle change that goes against societal norms.

Regardless of the scope of the decision, taking courageous steps requires us to confront our fears and step outside of our comfort zones. It can be scary to go against the grain and risk rejection or failure. However, it is often through these experiences that we grow and learn the most about ourselves.

One personal story of taking courageous steps that comes to mind is that of a friend who decided to leave their stable corporate job to start their own business. This was a significant risk, as they had a family to support and had no prior experience as an entrepreneur. However, they were passionate about their idea and believed that it had the potential to make a positive impact.

The journey was not easy. They faced financial setbacks, encountered resistance from potential investors, and had to learn a whole new set of skills to make their business successful. However, through their persistence and determination, they were able to build a thriving company that has now been in operation for several years.

Looking back on their decision, my friend reflects that taking courageous steps was one of the most challenging but also rewarding experiences of their life. They learned so much about themselves, their values, and what they are capable of achieving when they step outside of their comfort zone.

In conclusion, taking courageous steps and moving away from the herd is not always easy, but it can be a transformative experience that opens up new opportunities for growth and self-discovery. Whether we are inspired by the story of Rosa Parks or by the personal experiences of those around us, we can all find inspiration to take our own courageous steps and pursue our dreams, even if it means going against the norm.

Credits: Originated with CHATGPT AI, polished by Naishadh Gadani

CHATGTP is property of OpenAI

When have you taken steps of courage?

____

____

____

____

____

____

Written By

Naishadh Gadani
Engineer turned Career Practitioner. Author. Doodler. Presenter. Non-TEDx Speaker. Helping people design their careers.

How did it impact your career and life?

When you were not able to follow steps of courage? What stopped you?

Often opportunities
Seems scary !
But in reality they are NOT

Not Every Opportunity is Scary

This reflection is about an opportunity that brought about experiences that fulfilled me personally and professionally.

Context - My fear:

When I was in my 20s, I attempted a Doctorate in Organisational Psychology. I was close to the end, but then a thesis resubmission was required, and I never resubmitted. I spent my university life getting high grades in psychology, and I did not understand why I could not make the last hurdle. For years, this failure haunted me - the "what if?" questions would pour out, and I would create and recreate possibilities of what I could have done and become.

For years, it was one of my biggest regrets. However, in hindsight, my motivation to complete the doctorate was external - prestige around the qualification and university (it was reinforced to me as a teenager that the University of Melbourne was THE university to attend), and to make my parents proud of me. I did not have the motivation nor energy to continue; I didn't have any life or work experiences that were geared towards understanding organisational psychology - everything that I knew came from the books and articles I had read.

The Opportunity: Throughout the years, there were opportunities that I took, some I did not. However, there was one 'opportunity' that visited me during the pandemic. My manager approached me about applying for a scholarship to complete postgraduate research studies - at the time, I had started a Master's by coursework, and I was over halfway through. I enjoyed learning about education in this Master's, but it did not fulfill me academically. At the time, I didn't know this until the opportunity that visited me - I realised I wanted to be immersed in academia; I enjoyed reading research. I was the person or 'geek' at work that would explore the research to help me produce content on student employability.

When the opportunity arose to apply for the scholarship, I had to make a decision - should I continue with the Master's of Coursework that I was close to finishing or take a risk by applying for the Master of Research (scholarship) and subsequently discontinuing my current studies. Although I was eyeing the Master of Research, people would say to me, "But why not the PhD?" and then I would explain my history, kicking me in the gut every time I would retell my story. Honestly, I was intrigued by the possibility of completing a PhD, but I believed it was out of my reach and subsequently felt wary and scared.

How could I fail again?
Mindsets in grasping and using the Opportunity: I used the opportunity - the PhD project - as a way to research an area closer to my heart; I used my experiences as a former Arts student to determine who and what I wanted to research. Before I wrote my application for the scholarship, I was **curious** and reached out to a student through LinkedIn about their experience completing a program at the University of Texas that I had read about in The Conversation - this discussion partly instigated what I wanted to research. I used this action to take the opportunity and apply for the scholarship. I became successful. I took the **risk** and discontinued the Masters by coursework and enrolled in the PhD program.

I **reframed** the opportunity to do a PhD as a way to develop deep knowledge about pedagogy and employability and help other Arts graduates. I was able to use curiosity through my love of learning, into completing this PhD project (and I still am).

Through this opportunity, completing my PhD has opened up more pathways and enabled me to find further opportunities. I have been **curious** and have had the chance to meet many interesting and helpful people from around the world to learn about their educational programs. I approached this with an **open mind** and attended an international summer school for career research students in Kosovo, where I met many researchers and PhD students, some of whom have become friends. This opportunity also allowed me to **reframe** my previous failure into a positive light. All of the knowledge and skills I gained in my previous education and workplaces, such as writing research reports, reading about quantitative research, and performing statistical techniques and critiquing research, have provided me with many 'a-ha' moments in my current work as a PhD candidate, and I now have more confidence. By taking some **risks and being curious and open-minded,** I have been able to reframe the idea of completing a PhD from being scary and intimidating to being part of a process of human connections, learning, and personal fulfillment.

Written By

Freda Zapsalis
Careers Educator and PhD candidate at RMIT University. Using research to make a difference to student career development learning.

Write your reflections on the doodle.

Printed in Great Britain
by Amazon

23914779R00198